LIGHT FROM THE EAST

LIGHT FROM THE EAST

The Ecumenical Patriarch Bartholomew I

Michael O'Carroll, C.S.Sp.

Queenship
PUBLISHING COMPANY
P.O Box 42028 Santa Barbara, CA 93140-2028
(800) 647-9882 • (805) 957-4893 • Fax: (805) 957-1631

Dedication

To St. Joseph, Spouse of the Mother of God, Adoptive Father of Jesus Christ, Patron of the Universal Church, Patron of Workers: an act of reparation.

©1998 Queenship Publishing

Library of Congress Number # 98-65203

Published by:
Queenship Publishing
P.O. Box 42028
Santa Barbara, CA 93140-2028
(800) 647-9882 • (805) 957-4893 • Fax: (805) 957-1631

Printed in the United States of America

ISBN: 1-57918-062-0

Contents

Abbreviations

DC   *La Documentation Catholique*

ORE   *L'Osservatore Romano*, English weekly edition

PG   *Patrologia Graeca*

SP   *Service Orthodoxe de Presse*

Preface

I am honored to present to the reader the first substantial essay on the Ecumenical Patriarch of the Orthodox Church written by a priest of the Roman Catholic Church. Since I have published four books and many articles on the recent successors of Peter, especially the present Pope, John Paul II, it will be easily accepted that my intention is entirely ecumenical. For twenty years before Vatican II, I was involved in dialogue with Christians not of my communion. I have, in recent years, met members of the Orthodox Church in different countries, in Russia, Greece, Romania and elsewhere. I am, as are many others, immensely impressed by the revival of Orthodoxy around the world. In the presence of the spreading secularism and apostasy, it is a heartening sign.

Though I have given some pages of my book to Orthodoxy in its general features, its origin, history and present condition, my real hope is that it will be more fully understood through the personality of its present spiritual ruler, the Ecumenical Patriarch Bartholomew I - how precisely he is the spiritual ruler, is something to be known and appreciated by students of his Church.

I have not aimed at an exhaustive narrative of the Patriarch's activities during the six crowded years of his tenure of office. I have not reproduced the full text of all his pronouncements. I hope that what I have recorded illustrates his pastoral program. I intend to publish later a collection of his most important discourses and public statements.

I shall not conceal my disappointment at the attitude of my fellow Catholics towards the Orthodox Church. This attitude extends from theologians in important positions to the ordinary faithful. I have had to witness it in the preparatory phase of an important doctrinal statement by the Second Vatican Council, and in the life of the Church since then.

I have been very much encouraged by the policy of the present Pope in regard to the Orthodox. I hope that my Catholic readers will be helped to accept that it is in their interest that I seem to emphasize this aspect of my subject. Catholics need to know them. I have no doubt that they will benefit by the knowledge, all the more so, as they are following the example of their Pope.

Michael O'Carroll, C.S.Sp.
July 16, 1997, Feast of Our Lady of Mount Carmel

Chapter 1

The Orthodox Church

I

Catholic consciousness of the Orthodox Church as an important religious entity is one encouraging element in the contemporary situation. Down to the first decades of the present century the Orthodox, for Catholics, were largely unknown. After the Russian Revolution of 1917 and the Second World War, Orthodox Christians arrived in Europe and America and inevitably stirred interest and curiosity. History is taught in many ways. One is the witness of martyrs and here Orthodoxy was eloquent. In Russia alone, one hundred forty-thousand Orthodox priests, monks, nuns were the victims of the Stalinist regime. Add to that the figures amassed in the eastern European countries handed to Marxist regimes by the infamous Treaty of Yalta.

Another factor which focuses attention is powerful personality. Here too the Orthodox Church has excelled. From 1948 to 1972, the See of Constantinople (situated in modern Istanbul) was occupied by a spiritual giant, Athenagoras I.[1] He was already known in

---

[1] I had the honor, on June 24, 1967, of being received by the Patriarch, in his official residence, the Phanar, Istanbul. He had in his hand the telegram of thanks from Pope Paul VI, to whom he had sent greetings for his feast-day, St. John the Baptist. He expressed delight over the Pope's journey to Fatima—some Catholic progressive theologians had criticized Paul VI's decision. The Patriarch passed from grave to humorous in the course of our conversation over lunch. He spoke of his great hope: inter-communion. Teasingly, he asked if I knew who were the policeman in New York. I said, "Mostly Irish." "Yes, very upright men," was his comment.

the United States where he had been, for eighteen years, the ecclesiastical ruler of the Orthodox in that country. He eliminated the danger of schism and thoroughly organized the archdiocese. He was to figure in important inter-faith events which we shall consider. The world is indebted to him for drawing attention to the existence, scope and vitality of the Orthodox Church.

This Church commends itself to us first because of its antiquity. Our religion took its origin in the Eastern Mediterranean. Here the Orthodox Church has its roots. Its thinking is stimulated directly by the mighty minds of those who first reflected on the Christian revelation, those whom we call the Fathers of the Church, so many of them eastern. Its rule of faith is dictated by the first seven General Councils of the Church which took place in the East.

A Catholic should look for enlightenment on the Orthodox from the Teaching Authority of his Church. It is abundant and recent. Vatican II spoke thus on the Orthodox: "From their very origins the Churches of the East have had a treasury from which the Church of the West has drawn largely for its liturgy, spiritual tradition and jurisprudence. Nor must we underestimate the fact that the basic dogmas of the Christian faith concerning the Trinity and the Word of God made flesh from the Virgin Mary were defined in Ecumenical Councils held in the East. To preserve this faith these Churches have suffered, and still suffer much. Everyone knows with what love the Eastern Christians celebrate the sacred liturgy, especially the Eucharistic mystery, source of the Church's life and pledge of future glory...Hence through the celebration of the Eucharist of the Lord in each of these Churches, the Church of God is built up and grows in stature, and through concelebration, their communion with one another is made manifest.

"In this liturgical worship, the Eastern Christians pay high tribute, in hymns of praise, to Mary ever Virgin, whom the ecumenical Synod of Ephesus solemnly proclaimed to be the holy Mother of God in order that Christ might be truly acknowledged as Son of God and Son of Man, according to the scriptures. They also give homage to the saints, among them the Fathers of the universal Church. Moreover, in the East are to be found the riches of those spiritual traditions, which are given expression in monastic life especially."

The Council points out that monastic spirituality flourished in the East "from the glorious times of the holy Fathers: and "later flowed over into the western world, and there provided a source from which Latin monastic life took its rise, and has often drawn fresh vigor ever since."[2]

II

Thus spoke the Fathers of Vatican II on November 21, 1964. The reader will now profit by reading a joint declaration in Rome by the Pope of the Council, Paul VI, and the Orthodox leader already mentioned, Athenagoras I.[3] They had met in Jerusalem in 1964 when the Patriarch, true to his statement of purpose on the news of John XXIII's announcement of a General Council, had taken the initiative, the first in history, of flying there to meet the Pope. Now on December 7, 1965 both prelates had agreed on this historical statement:

1. Full of gratitude to God for the favor which is mercifully granted them in their brotherly meeting in those holy places where the mystery of our salvation was accomplished by the death and resurrection of the Lord Jesus, and where the Church was born by the outpouring of the Holy Spirit, Pope Paul VI

---

[2] *Decree on Ecumenism*, 14, 15.

[3] Patriarch Athenagoras who had sent a warm message, through the Associated Press, on hearing the announcement of a Council, said in his New Year address that Christian leaders had to reconsider their common duty to affirm the primacy of the Spirit: "Therefore in deepest consciousness of this duty we declare the sincere willingness of our Orthodox Church to continue in prayer and supplication for the peace of the whole world; to cooperate positively in practical ways for the advancement of the cause of Christian unity..." He saw in the Pope's appeal an echo of ancient times when people turned towards the East. "This we wish and expect from His Holiness, the new Pope of Rome, John XXIII, who is well-known in our churchly jurisdictions, and this wish is not ours alone but it is the expectation of Christians who hope to see the dawn of a real New Year in Christ." Great men learn from experience: John XXIII had spent twenty years in the Near East in Bulgaria and Turkey, a witness to divided Christendom; Athenagoras saw the effects of disunity during eighteen years in the United States; cf. M.O'Carroll, *Pope John XXIII*, Dublin, 1959 pp. 110-113.

and Patriarch Athenagoras I have not lost sight of the intention which they held from then onwards, each for his part, never to omit in the future any of those gestures inspired by charity which might contribute towards the fraternal relationships thus initiated between the Roman Catholic Church and the Orthodox Church of Constantinople. They believe that they are thus responding to the call of divine grace, which today requires that the Roman Catholic Church and the Orthodox Church, as well as all Christians, overcome their differences, so as to be again 'one' as the Lord Jesus had asked of His Father for them.

2. Among the obstacles to be found in the way of the development of these brotherly relationships of trust and esteem, there is the memory of those painful decisions, acts and incidents which led in 1054 to the sentence of excommunication delivered against Patriarch Michael Cerularius and two other persons by the legates of the Roman See led by Cardinal Humbert, legates who were themselves in turn objects of a similar sentence on the side of the Patriarch and the Synod of Constantinople.

3. One cannot pretend that these events were not what they were in that particularly troubled period of history. But now that today a more calm and equitable judgment has been brought to bear on them, it is important to recognize the excesses with which they were tainted and which later led to consequences which, as far as we can judge, went much further then their authors had intended or expected; they were not meant to break ecclesiastical communion between the Sees of Rome and Constantinople.

4. That is why Pope Paul VI and Patriarch Athenagoras I with his synod, certain that they are expressing the common desire for justice and the unanimous sentiment of charity on the part of their faithful, and remembering the command of the Lord: 'If you are offering your gift at the altar, and then remember that your brother has something against you, leave your gift before

the altar and go first to be reconciled to your brother' (Mt 5:23-24), declare with one accord that:

(a) They regret the offensive words, the reproaches without foundation and the reprehensible gestures which, on both sides, marked or accompanied the sad events of that period;

(b) They also regret and wish to erase from the memory and midst of the Church the sentences of excommunication which followed them, and whose memory has acted as an obstacle to a rapprochement in charity down to our day, and to consign them to oblivion;

(c) Finally, they deplore the troublesome precedents and the later events which, under the influence of various factors, among them lack of understanding and mutual hostility, eventually led to the effective rupture of ecclesiastical communion.

5. This reciprocal act of justice and forgiveness, as Pope Paul VI and Patriarch Athenagoras I with his synod are aware, cannot suffice to put an end to the differences, ancient or more recent, which remain between the Roman Catholic Church and the Orthodox Church and which, by the action of the Holy Spirit, will be overcome, thanks to the purification of hearts, regret for historical errors, and an effective determination to arrive at a common understanding and expression of the apostolic faith and its demands.

In accomplishing this act, however, they hope that it will be pleasing to God, who is prompt to pardon us when we forgive one another, and recognized by the whole Christian world, but especially by the Roman Catholic Church and the Orthodox Church together, as the expression of a sincere mutual desire for reconciliation and as an invitation to pursue, in a spirit of mutual trust, esteem and charity, the dialogue which will lead them, with the help of God, to live once again for the greater good of souls and the coming of the Kingdom of God, in the full communion of faith, of brotherly concord and of a sacramental life which existed between them throughout the first millennium of the life of the Church.[4]

III

Commentary on this document will enlighten the reader on the Orthodox Church. In the first millennium of Christianity the Church was one in belief and practice, with legitimate diversity locally. Government was seen in a pentarchy, exercised by five supreme rulers, acknowledged as patriarchs, Jerusalem, Antioch, Alexandria, Constantinople and Rome.

Vatican II thus describes this situation: "For many centuries, the Churches of the East and of the West went their own ways, though a brotherly communion of faith and sacramental life bound them together. If disagreements in belief and discipline arose among them, the Roman See acted by common consent as moderator.[5] This was recognition of the Roman Pontiff as *primus inter pares*. Jerusalem, Antioch and Alexandria claimed origin from the Apostles. There had been, with the passage of time, shifts in intellectual leadership. In the early centuries with the Christians of Rome subject to the almost uninterrupted pressure of persecution, intellect at the service of the faith was mostly in the East, with Alexandria in a dominant role: it had the first great Christian library, the first Catechetical School and its intellectuals helped powerfully to orient and deepen Christian thought and provide a bulwark against heresy.

It is important to recall the names of the great teachers and doctors of Alexandria in any consideration of the Orthodox Church, rejoicing in the fact that with the recent revival of patristic studies in the West there will be, as Pope John Paul II has pointed out, awareness of how much East and West owe them; this should foster our sense of unity. The great names are St. Clement (d. 215), Origen (d. 254) St. Alexander(d.328), and St. Athanasius (d.373), Didymus the Blind (d.398), and St. Cyril (d.444). Origen was one

---

[4] Text reproduced in *Vatican Council II, Conciliar and Post-Conciliar Documents*, ed. Austin Flannery, O.P., Dublin, 1975, pp. 471-473.

[5] *Op.cit.,* 14.

of the most prolific writers of the early centuries: Athanasius and Cyril had essential roles in epoch-making Councils: Nicaea and Ephesus respectively. The abundance of talent and commitment in this one city is mentioned to stimulate interest in the entire patristic legacy which inspires and sustains the Orthodox Church.

What are the distinctive features to be noted and admired in the Church so intellectually nourished? Again, we have guidance from our own Teaching Authority, in this case an Apostolic Letter, *Orientale Lumen* May 3, 1995, from our present Pope, who is known to have given much time to the study of the Orthodox Church; the evidence of this interest and acquisition has been seen in the weekly issues of *L'Osservatore Romano* in recent years.

The Pope begins with this assertion: "A particularly close link already binds us. We have almost everything in common; and above all, we have in common the true longing for unity."

Later, he has this to say: "Pondering over the questions, aspirations and experiences I have mentioned, my thoughts turn to the Christian heritage of the East. I do not intend to describe or to interpret it: I listen to the Churches of the East, which I know are living interpreters of the treasure of tradition they preserve. In contemplating it, before my eyes appear elements of great significance for a fuller and more thorough understanding of the Christian experience. These elements are capable of giving a more complete Christian response to the expectations of the men and women of today. Indeed, in comparison to any other culture, the Christian East has a unique and privileged role as to the original setting where the Church was born."

The Pope continues to insist on Tradition. This is basic to all Orthodox thinking; indeed one Orthodox theologian, Sergius Bulgakov, has gone so far as to say that Sacred Scripture is included in Tradition. The goal, says the Pope is: "participation in the divine nature through communion with the mystery of the Holy Trinity." Then he brings up a most important truth, not only in Orthodox thought or belief, but in the spiritual life as wholly seen: the Holy Spirit. "Participation in Trinitarian life takes place through the liturgy and in a special way through the Eucharist, mystery of communion with the glorified body of Christ, the seed of immortality. In divinization and particularly the sacraments, Eastern theology attributes a very special role to the Holy Spirit: through the power of the Spirit who dwells in man deification already begins on earth; the creature is transfigured and God's kingdom inaugurated. The teaching of the Cappadocian Fathers on divinization passed into the tradition of all the Eastern Churches and is part of their common heritage. This can be summarized in the thought already expressed by Saint Irenaeus at the end of the second century: *God passed into man so that man might pass over to God.* This theology of divinization remains one of the achievements particularly dear to Eastern Christian thought."

The Pope then points out that "although strongly emphasizing Trinitarian realism and its unfolding in sacramental life, the East associates faith in the unity of the divine nature with the fact that the divine essence is unknowable. The Eastern Fathers always assert that it is impossible to know what God is; one can only known that He is, since He revealed Himself in the history of salvation as Father, Son and Holy Spirit." The Pope adds that this "sense of mystery" is strongly felt in "the liturgical celebration."

IV

Inculturation is a theme and problem central almost to present day evangelization. John Paul II makes clear that it was wonderfully achieved by the Orthodox and he evokes again the idea of Tradition, basic to all Orthodox theology and spirituality: "Only a religious assimilation, in the obedience of faith, of what the Church calls 'Tradition' will enable Tradition to be embodied in different cultural and historical situations and conditions. Tradition is never pure nostalgia for things or forms past, nor regret for lost privileges, but the living memory of the Bride, kept eternally youthful by the Love that dwells within her."

Going on to another idea John Paul says: "If Tradition puts us in continually with the past, eschatological expectation opens us to God's future...The East expresses in a living way the reality of Tradition and expectation. All its liturgy, in particular, is a commemoration of salvation and an invocation of the Lord's return. And if Tradition teaches the Churches' fidelity to what gave birth to them, *eschatological expectation urges them to be what they have not yet fully become*, what the Lord wants them to become, and thus to seek ever new ways of fidelity, overcoming pessimism because they are striving for the hope of God who does not disappoint. We must show people the beauty of memory, the power that comes to us from the Spirit and makes us witnesses because *we are children of witnesses*; we must make them taste the wonderful things the Spirit has wrought in history; we must show that it is precisely Tradition which has preserved them, thus giving hope to those who, even without seeing their efforts to do good crowned by success, know that someone else will bring them to fulfillment; therefore man will be less alone, less enclosed in a narrow corner of his own individual achievement.

Pope John Paul is enthusiastic in his praise of Eastern monasticism, which, as he says, has "always been the very soul of the Eastern Churches" — he speaks of "the splendid witness of nuns of the Christian East." Monasticism, the Pope thinks, will help him "to identify those values which I feel are very important today for expressing the contribution of the Christian East to the journey of Christ's Church towards the Kingdom."

No Pope has spoken like this about Orthodox spiritual life. Nor has any so lauded Eastern devotion to the Eucharist. This leads him to offer some enlightening reflections on the liturgy.

"In the liturgical experience, Christ the Lord is the light which illumines the way and reveals the transparency of the cosmos, precisely as in Scripture. The events of the past find in Christ their meaning and fullness, and creation is revealed for what it is: a complex whole which finds its perfection, its purpose *in the liturgy* alone. This is why the liturgy is heaven on earth, and in it the Word who became flesh imbues matter with a saving potential which is fully manifest in the sacraments: there, creation communicates to each individual the power conferred on it by Christ. ...Within this framework liturgical prayer in the East shows a great aptitude for involving the human person in his or her totality; the mystery is sung in the loftiness of its content, but also in the warmth of the sentiments it awakens in the heart of redeemed humanity. In the sacred act, even bodiliness is summoned to praise, and beauty, which in the East is one of the best-loved names expressing the divine harmony and the model of humanity transfigured, appears everywhere: in the shape of the church, in the sounds, in the colors, in the lights, in the scents. The lengthy duration of the celebrations, the repeated invocations, everything expresses gradual identification with the mystery celebrated with one's whole person."

V

Another aspect of the Orthodox liturgy appeals strongly to the Pope: "Cosmic reality also is summoned to give thanks because the whole universe is called to recapitualization in Christ the Lord. This concept expresses a balanced and marvelous teaching on the dignity , respect and purpose of creation and of the human body in particular. With the rejection of all dualism and every cult of pleasure as an end in itself, the body becomes a place made luminous by grace thus fully human."[6]

Elsewhere John Paul II has drawn attention to the profound Christian anthropology taught by the Orthodox. Here he was possibly influenced not only by biblical reflection but by his expertise in phenomenology which is recognized in an important *Dictionnaire des Philosophes* issued in France. "A certain trend," he says, "in humanistic culture has led many men and women of our time to turn away from God. But with the decline of the great ideologies, it has become dramatically clear that when man becomes 'bereft of God,' he loses the meaning of his own life and in some way becomes bereft' of himself. Who is man? Christianity, in its two-fold tradition of East and West, has always taken this question seriously. It has given rise to a profound, harmonious anthropology based on the principle that the ultimate truth of the human being is to be sought in the One who created him.

"Eastern spirituality makes a specific contribution to authentic knowledge of man by insisting on the perspective of the heart. Christians of the East love to distinguish three types of knowledge. The first is limited to man in his bio-psychic structure. The second remains in the realm of moral life. The highest degree of self-knowledge is obtained, however, in contemplation, by which man returns deeply into himself, recognizes himself as the divine image

---

[6] CTS edition.

and, purifying himself of sin, meets the living God to the point of becoming 'divine' himself by the gift of grace.

"This is knowledge of the heart. Here the 'heart' means much more than a human faculty, such as affectivity, for example. It is rather the principle of personal unity, a sort of 'interior space' in which the person recollects his whole self so as to live in the knowledge and love of the Lord."[7]

A member of the Latin Church is prompted by such teaching to look for a possible analogy in western theology or spirituality. The obvious theme is that of the Sacred Heart of Jesus and the Immaculate Heart of Mary. The theology of the Sacred Heart, stimulated undoubtedly by private revelation is taking on a powerful new dimension from deeper understanding of the Old Testament. These writings disclose the third and greatest civilization of the ancient Mediterranean, that of the heart, statement of the person, opening to the Creator a civilization superior to that of the intellect from Greece and to one based on law, the achievement of Rome.

With the full, explicit recognition, in our time, of the Jewishness of Jesus, we may look to the civilization within which he was born for understanding of his thought. He was, is and ever shall be, a Jew with all the splendor of that inheritance. The sacred books of the Old Testament speak eight hundred and fifty times of the heart. St. Thomas Aquinas thought that the fifth beatitude, "Blessed are the pure of heart," could summarize the whole Gospel of Jesus Christ: purity of heart is a basic Old Testament theme.

One cannot push these suggestions on a possible synthesis of Old Testament, Orthodox and Roman Catholic thought too far; there is need for much reflection and research.

VI

Mary in Orthodox doctrine and piety is a theme to stir the greatest hope in the hearts of those who long for Christian unity. The *Theotokos*, Mother of God, is variously depicted in the icons and we know, and shall again recall, the importance of icons in the Orthodox world, most perfect is Our Lady of Vladimir now brought

---

[7] ORE.

from its exile in the Tretiakov Museum in Moscow to its rightful home, the Church of the Assumption inside the Kremlin. The liturgy proclaims Mary's greatness and her glory. An expert has declared that the Byzantine Liturgy of Our Lady is the most perfect composed anywhere in her honor.

The Orthodox liturgies, a prime source for their theology in the expression of Tradition, reveal the cosmic design realized in Christ, exalt the Passion and its symbol, the Cross, and rise to sublime heights in chanting the Resurrection. Let us quote from the great anaphora of the Byzantine Liturgy of St. Basil. After a sublime passage addressed to the Father extolling Christ in his wondrous attributes and his sending of the Spirit we have these beautiful words: "He, the brightness of your glory, the impress of your substance, sustaining all things by the word of his power, counted it not a prize to be an equality with you, O God, his Father. Himself, eternal God, he appeared on earth and lived among men; becoming incarnate of the holy Virgin, he emptied himself by taking the form of a slave, being made in his body like us, that he might make us like to the image of his glory. For since sin had entered the world through man, and death through sin, your only-begotten Son though being in your bosom, O God his Father, was born of a woman, the holy Mother of God and ever-virgin Mary, born under the law, in order to condemn sin in his flesh, so that those who were dead in Adam might in him, your Christ, be made alive."[8]

The Easter Matins contain a wonderful hymn of praise: "Glorify him O my soul, who is risen from the tomb on the third day, the life-giving Christ! Shine, new Jerusalem, shine for the glory of the Lord is risen on you. Zion, rejoice and be glad. And you, holy Mother of God, rejoice, for your Son is risen...An angel cried to the Virgin blest: 'Rejoice, unsullied Maiden! Again I say, Rejoice! Your son in very truth is risen. Three days was He in the tomb, and now is risen from the dead.'"

In these words we have, in the Orthodox manner, the idea of Mary's participation in the total Paschal Mystery, what we should perhaps name her role as Co-Redemptress. What of her interces-

---

[8]   *Byzantine Liturgy of St. Basil*, apud M.J.le Guillou, O.P., Faith and Fact Books, 136, *The Tradition of Eastern Orthodoxy*, London, 1962, 42 sq.

sion, her role as Advocate? Let us turn to the Divine Liturgy of St. John Chrysostom. Here, in the Liturgy of Catechumens we read: "Remembering our most holy, pure, blessed and glorious Lady, the Theotokos and every virgin Mary, with all the saints, let us commit ourselves and one another and our whole life to Christ our God."

These are the words of the priest. For the first antiphon the people cry, "By the intercession of the Theotokos, Saviour save us." This is then repeated twice; the priest repeats his invocation later. We come to the Liturgy of the Faithful, to the anaphora. The priest having incensed the offerings, now by his words consecrated to the Body and Blood of Christ prays thus: "Especially for our most holy, pure, blessed and glorious Lady, the Theotokos and ever virgin Mary." To this the people reply; "It is truly right to bless you, Theotokos, ever blessed, most pure and Mother of our God. More honorable than the Cherubim, and beyond compare more glorious than the Seraphim, without corruption you gave birth to God the Word. We magnify you, the true Theotokos."[9]

Our Lady is thus mentioned at the heart of the Eucharistic celebration.[10] It would be illuminating to pursue this theme through the liturgy, with special attention to the Akathistos Hymn, originating centuries before the break in Christian unity, given a very important place in Orthodox liturgy.

It will probably be more helpful for the reader to delay on a great age in Orthodox theology when the Palamite teachers and preachers flourished. Take this passage from St. Gregory Palamas (d.1359) from whom they get their name: "Mary is the cause of what had gone before her, the pioneer of what has come after here; she distributes eternal goods; she is the thought of the prophets, the head of the Apostles, the support of martyrs, the certainty of doctors. She is the glory of earth, the joy of heaven, the ornament of all

---

[9] *The Divine Liturgy of St. John Chrysostom*, ed. Professor Ion Bria, World Council of Churches, 4,18.

[10] At the end, before distributing the blessed bread, the priest says: "May Christ, our true God (who rose from the dead) as a good, loving and merciful God, have mercy upon us and save us, through the intercession of His most pure and holy Mother (other motives are added), Ibid. 28.

creation. She is the principle, the source, the root of ineffable good things. She is the summit and fulfillment of all that is holy."[11]

Mary, Gregory thought, was on the confines of the created and the uncreated; she stands alone between God and the whole human race. She made God the Son of man and men the sons of God. Gregory thought that all the divinely-inspired Scripture was written because of the Virgin, who brought forth God. His idea of Mary's mediation is implicit in his view of her cosmic role. He made it explicit in this passage: "No divine gift can reach either angels or men, save through her mediation. As one cannot enjoy the light of a lamp...save through the medium of the lamp, so every movement towards God, every impulse towards good coming from Him, is unrealizable save through the mediation of the Virgin. She does not cease to spread benefits on all creatures, not only on men but on 'celestial incorporeal ranks.'"[12]

Before continuing I should state the reason for delaying on the Orthodox theologians of Mary's mediation. First, I wish to make amends to our brethren of the East for the neglect of this splendid doctrinal corpus by the commission charged with drafting the Marian chapter of the Constitution on the Church in Vatican II. A great Orientalist, Fr. Antoine Wenger, A.A., submitted a memorandum to the commission on the importance of the idea in Eastern theology. He was "called to moderation" by the commission secretary, Fr. Moeller. There was worse to follow. In the guidelines circulated to the Council Fathers it was stated that the Eastern theologians, while using the title "do not construct a theological system." This was not the only serious error in their assertion; they also claimed that Pius XII never used the title: he did so eight times![13]

I should answer this grave error while omitting three other fourteenth century Orthodox theologians who could be invoked against it;

---

[11] *In Assumpt.*, pg 151, 177B.

[12] Ed. of Sophocles Oikonomos, Athens, 1861, 159; pg. 151, 472A.

[13] References in regard to Fr. Wenger and Pius XII in articles, "Mediation," 238-245, and "Pius XIII," 290-291, M.O'Carroll, *Theotokos* Wilmington, 1982 and subsequent editions; cf. M.O'Carroll, C.S.Sp.; cf. M.O'Carroll, "Mary, as Coredemptrix, Mediatrix and Advocate, Instrument of Catholic-Orthodox Unity," in *Mary, Coredemptris, Mediatrix, Advocate*, ed. Mark Miravalle, Queenship Publishing Co., 1995, 119-143.

I have dealt elsewhere with them: Nicephorus Callistus (d.1335), Nicholas Cabasilas (d.1322) and Isidore Glabas (d.1397).[14] I wish to deal with the greatest exponent of Mary's mediation in this Golden Age of Orthodox Theology, given the name Palamite from St. Gregory: Theophenes of Nicaea (d.1381), author of a sermon, which is a treatise on the subject, magnificently structured, admirably systematic. He is, in the opinion of an eminent Marian theologian, Fr. Martin Jugie, A.A., the greatest teacher of Mary's universal mediation, which is to say that he surpasses St. Germanus of Constantinople (d.733) in the East and in the West St. Bernard (d.1153), St. Louis Marie Grignion de Montfort (d.1716) and St. Alphonsus de Liguori (d. 1787).

VII

Theophanes is not only the answer to the conciliar draftsmen who asserted that the Eastern theologians do not construct a system on Our Lady's mediation. He deserves to be at the very center of the worldwide campaign now being conducted to secure a Marian dogma on Mary, Coredemptress, Mediatress, Advocate. When the Father has heard the prayer of His divine Son, Theophanes will be fully recognized as an instrument in the blessed achievement: "I do not pray for these only, but also for those who believe in me through their word, that they may all be one; even as thou, Father, art in me, and I in thee, that they also may be one in us, so that the world may believe that thou hast sent me. The glory which though hast given me I have given to them, that they may be one even as we are one. I in them and thou in me, that they may become perfectly one, so that the world may know that thou hast sent me and hast loved them even as thou has loved me." (Jn. 17:20-23)

Theophanes linked his idea with the absolute primacy of Christ in creation, and with the Orthodox basic theme of divinization by divine grace. God the Word shared our flesh and blood and through him we become sharers in His divine nature. Who, He asks, was the intermediary, who provided the means for this wondrous exchange? "Truly this was the Virgin and Mother of God. For through her we gave our nature to God the Word; therefore the divinity that is be-

---

[14] Cf. articles under these names in *Theotokos*.

stowed on us truly through her is given. Just as she gave our nature directly to God the Word, so God the Word directly to her repaid the deification of all; just as the Son of God through the mediation of his own Mother received from us our nature, so through her mediation we receive his deification. It is therefore impossible that anyone in any way may become a sharer in the gifts of God other than in the way that we have set forth."[15]

Theophanes uses, in an exalted way, a metaphor current among Latin writers, Mary as the neck of the Mystical Body, "pleasing to God and illuminated by the rays of the Holy Spirit." He reflects on and analyses penetratingly the relationship between Mary and each of the divine Persons; his pages on the Holy Spirit meet a crying need in the Church today, "The Mother of the Son is the image of the Paraclete, not really a natural one, but by participation and grace, in such wise that incomparably above all created nature, she represents the prototype, and in her alone most eminently shine and are beheld all the graces and splendors of the Spirit related to her Son."[16]

Finally, one quotation to show the great Marian theologian's grasp of the spiritual motherhood, as well as his clear teaching on Mary as the dispenser of all graces: "The Mother of him who through his unspeakable goodness willed to be called our brother is the dispenser and distributor of all the wondrous uncreated gifts of the divine Spirit, which make us Christ's brothers and co-heirs, not only because she is granting the gifts of her natural Son to his brothers in grace, but also because she is bestowing them on these as her own true sons, though not by ties of nature but of grace."[17] Theophanes rightly thinks we owe Mary praise and virtue in imitation of her. Praise is certainly due to Theophanes himself; his magnificently ar-

---

[15] *Sermo in Sanctissimam Deiparam*, Lateranum, Nova Series, 1, Rome 1935. "On Theophanes" cf. M.O'Carroll, *Theotokos*, 340 sq and in *Dictionnaire de Spiritualite*, XV, 516 sq bibliography to each article. "On Martin Jugie, the Greatest Catholic Prientalist of Modern Times" cf. *Theotokos*, 210. Of the many eastern works published by Fr. Jugie for the first time, this is the most important. It has not been appreciated, or even known by many western theologians, including the drafting commission of the Marian Chapter of *Lumen Gentium*, as has been stated; *op. cit.*, V, p. 51.

[16] *Op. cit.* XIII, 193.

[17] *Op. cit.*, XV, 205.

gued treastise, unknown until 1935, merits the epithet sublime. It should give thought to the ill-informed among our Catholic brethren who do not know of the immense treasures of doctrine wrought and transmitted in the Orthodox Church. When the dogma of Mary's universal mediation is proclaimed one of the principal witnesses cited to Tradition will be this mighty theologian of the Orthodox Church.

VIII

To the body of the faithful and to those led to a deeper communion with the Christian mystery, icons are a precious means of acquiring theological awareness. It was at the Second Council of Nicaea in 787, that the controversy about icons was settled; it had in places raged. The solemnity of a General Council, the last of the seven acknowledged by the Orthodox, invested these religious products with a specially sacred character. They are not only venerated, but seen as something like a sacramental. Whereas Our Lady appears personally to individuals in the Latin Church, often she signifies her presence to Orthodox faithful through the icons, which may become luminous or exude oil — of this latter phenomenon there are contemporary examples verified.

Ideally, icons are created in strict conformity with Tradition, free of commercialism in obedience to strict rules. They figure in great movements, as Our Lady of Khazan, awaiting in Fatima its return to its rightful home in Moscow. They are in Byzantine churches displayed on the partition of wood or stone which separates the sanctuary from the nave, which takes its name, Iconostasis from them. They inspire theologians, like Soloviev and Florenski, especially in the case of Sergius Bulgakov, who begins one of his great works with a reflection on the Icon of Our Lady of Novgorod. Publicly known miracles are associated on the Icon of Our Lady of Novgorod. Publicly known miracles are associated with icons, that of Christ of Edessa, said not to be the product of human hands, or of the Theotokos in the monastery of the Abramites in Constantinople. Icons of Our Lady are distinguished in different kinds: a) the *Kyriotissa*, or Virgin in majesty, with which is linked the *Nicopea*, the one who gives victory; b) the *Blachernitissa*, the Virgin praying, deriving from the ancient shrine of Blakhernae in Constantinople; c) the *Haghiosoritissa*, originating in the shrine of Our Lady's Girdle or *Zona*, a relic left by

Byzantines and glorified by preachers and poets; d) the *Hodegetria*, Guide of the Way, which name is of unknown origin, but the icons so grouped are many, and widespread, even as far as Italy; e) the *Eleousa*, the Mother of Tenderness, the type exemplified in the supreme instance of the icon, Our Lady of Vladmir. Associated with this type is the *Strastnaia*, the Sorrowing Virgin, exemplified in an icon well-known to Catholics, *Our Lady of Perpetual Help,* honored in the Redemptorist Church in Rome; the *Glycophilousa*, the Virgin kissing the Child's hand; the *Galactotrephousa*, the Virgin giving milk to the Divine Child; the *Virgin Source of Life*, and the *Pokrov*, the Protectress, a favorite with the Russians. An authority on the subject has given as his opinion that the two greatest icons are *Our Lady of Vladimir* — to which John Paul II referred in his Encyclical on Our Lady, *Redemptoris Mater*, and Rublev's *Trinity*. Both were housed as museum pieces, in the Tretiakov, Moscow, but untouched as many churches, those inside the Kremlin and St. Basil's on Red Square were allowed to remain — others were destroyed or turned to secular use. Thanks to the permanent aura of reverence surrounding icons, they have been spared the kind of vandalism recently turned against images and statues, especially of Our Lady, in some Catholic churches.

IX

The reader who has not had the opportunity to acquire very much knowledge of Orthodoxy may feel prompted on reading the high praise of this Church so far set forth from papal writing or pronouncements to ask such questions as these:

How did the separation between Orthodox and Roman Catholics occur and why has it been perpetuated?

How does the Orthodox Church exist as a structured ecclesiastical body, in comparison with the Roman Catholic Church and, say, the Anglican and Lutheran and Calvinist ecclesial communities?

What signs are there of vitality and growth in the Orthodox Church?

What is the foundation for hope for future unity between Catholics and Orthodox?

The mutual acts of excommunication of 1054, revoked solemnly by Pope Paul VI and Patriarch Athenagoras, are taken as the breaking point between East and West. There had been some tension before that but the clash between the Patriarch of Constantinople, Michael Cerularius, and the Papal Legate, Cardinal Humbert, has for historians justified fixing a date; it does not mean that the separation was total.[18] The incident assumed, with the passage of time, more importance that was inherent in it. Michael Cerularius was sensitive to any Roman attempt to restrict his power. Cardinal Humbert of Moyenmoutier was a man with little finesse and an obstinate character. In the face of the Patriarch's suspicion of papal interference, and conscious of Byzantine polemics, he threatened that the Eastern Church would, if it did not submit to the Pope's authority, become nothing more than "an assembly of heretics, a conventicle of schismatics and a synagogue of Satan." Scarcely the language of Christian love, which should animate diplomacy as well as everyday living.

Michael Cerularius refused to deal with the Legate, who on July 16 formally excommunicated him in Santa Sofia's. This he had no authority to do; it exceeded his brief. The Patriarch answered with anathemas against the Legate. Thus, a certain alienation which had gone on for some time was hardened. Efforts would be made to restore unity, but decisions taken at the Councils of Lyons in 1274 and at Florence in 1439 were not effective throughout the Orthodox Church; things remained as they were.

One disastrous event embittered profoundly relations between East and West. Encouraged by the powerful medieval Pope, Innocent III, a Crusade set out in 1202 with the same objective as the previous crusades: to liberate the Holy Places. Through the influence of the Venetians and Boniface of Montserrat it turned aside to Constantinople. The city, capital of the Orthodox Church, was cap-

---

[18] The name of Photius (d.c.895), a controversial Patriarch is occasionally recalled as a sign of the conflict between East and West. The reader is referred to a basic work, F.Dvornik, *The Photian Schism, History and Legend*, 1948; the same author in N.C.E. XI, 326-9. The encyclopedic knowledge of Photius was in two points to leave a lasting effect, the pamphlet *Against Those Who Say That Rome is the Premier See* and *Treatise on the Holy Spirit*. In the latter work he criticized the Latin Church for the edition of the *Filioque* to the Creed; his work was to become the quarry for future anti-Roman polemicists. One must also note a political irritant in a world where Church and State were closely allied. It was a grievance of the eastern imperial set that Rome was allied with the Ottos, the German emperors in the West, successors to Charlemagne, whose coronation by the Pope in 800 A.D. had displeased Constantinople.

tured, ransacked and looted. A Latin kingdom was established and a Latin Patriarch installed; the kingdom lasted from 1204 to 1261. The Pope accepted this order of things; it has never been forgotten in the East — how could it? Without help from the West which the Council of Florence seemed to promise, but in vain, the capital city of the Orthodox world fell to the Turks — two hundred thirty years later they were at the gates of Vienna, the last obstacle to their advance into Italy; here they were halted by the Polish king John Sobieski and his ally, John of Lorraine. The Patriarch of Constantinople has remained within the Turkish world since 1453.

His flock in Turkey, at one time 100,000, has declined to a little over 3,000. His status has remained unchanged among the Orthodox worldwide, surviving a brief challenge from Moscow. He is the first of the four great patriarchs, first in honor, *primus inter pares*, his title Ecumenical Patriarch. The three other patriarchates claming apostolic origin are those of Jerusalem, Antioch and Alexandria. The dignity of each is understood in the light of the shift in power from Rome to the East and to decisions taken in the first General Council all of which were held in the East, all summoned by the Emperor.

Four other patriarchates have been recognized with the passage of time: Bulgarian (917); Serbian (1346); Russian (1589); Romanian (1925). The Church in Georgia is styled a Catholicate, ruled by a Catholicos. Six other Churches, entirely self-governing, are styled autocephalous: Cyprus (431); Sinai (1575); Greece (1830); Poland (1924); Albania (1937); Czechoslovakia (1951). Churches attached to the great patriarchates, autonomous but not autocephalous are those in Finland, Estonia, Latvia, Hungary, China, Japan, Macedonia, North America, three Russian churches outside the homeland, Ukrainians and Ruthenians abroad.

Just as the Orthodox cling tenaciously to the idea of Tradition, so do they insist on the importance of conciliar, that is collective action in the life of the Church. The whole Church must be brought into decisions and doctrinal positions.

X

The present state of the Orthodox Church throughout the world is of immediate interest to all who watch the evolving picture of religion in our time. The dominant note is optimistic. Orthodoxy is entering, has entered, a phase of revival. Most striking is the resurgence in countries which have passed through persecution. Russia suffered heavily in this ordeal. Some statistics will enlighten.

We have had recently the first religious statistics published since 1915. At the time of the Russian Christian Millennium in 1988 there were 6,800 parishes; now there are 15,810. Eparchies (dioceses) have increased from 47 to 114. There are now in the Russian Orthodox Church 136 diocesan and auxiliary bishops, 12,707 priests and 1,380 deacons. Almost half the 269 monasteries have reopened since 1992. There are 2,548 candidates for the priesthood studying in 13 seminaries.

Inevitably, there must be comparison with pre-Revolutionary Russia. Then there were 54,000 parishes, over 50,000 parish schools, over 1,000 monasteries and 40 seminaries. I have mentioned the victims of persecution whose sacrifice made this revival possible. One is reminded of the flowering of religious, especially missionary congregations in France, after the Revolution, the divine answer to the Reign of Terror in which the Church suffered so heavily.

A striking revival is also under way in Romania, which has after Russia the largest Orthodox population. It must surely interest students of the consecrated, religious life in Europe to know that there are convents of nuns with over 300 members.

Before the Revolution, religion, that is Orthodoxy, had influenced the great Russian writers, Dostoievsky (d.1881) and Tolstoy (d.1910). A friend of Dostoievsky, Vladimir Solovieff (d.1900) looked to a union of Christians. A writer of great stature, he has been styled "A Russian Newman"; eventually he was received into the Catholic Church.[19]

---

[19] Among Orthodox writers to note are in the English-speaking world Archbishop Anthony Bloom, an esteemed spiritual author and on the world scene one of the heroes of our time, Alexander Solshenitsyn, who revealed the grim reality of the Gulag and made public two letters which shine in the treasury of Christian heroism: an open letter to the Patriarch requesting support for those who had their children baptized—this was before Glasnost and Perestroika, and an open letter to the rulers of Russia in which he stated bluntly "Marxism had been the economic ruin of our country."

The triumph of Stalin drove the Russian Orthodox intellectuals abroad. Their greatest rallying center was the St. Serge Institute, founded in Paris in 1925. There we meet a succession of great names in theology who commanded respect widely: George Florovsky (d.1974), Vladimir Lossky (d.1958), Sergius Bulgakov (d.1944), Paul Evdokimov (d.1970), Nicholas Berdyaev (d. 1948). Another higher institute which provided intellectual stimulus to the Orthodox and transmitted their theological ideas was St. Vladimir's Seminary in New York. Its great luminary was John Meyerndorff, who died recently. His great triumph, apart from demonstrating the solid intellectual fabric of Orthodox theology, was the discovery of a great Orthodox theologian of the fourteenth century, Gregory Palamas (d.1359), a principal exponent of the Special Orthodox form of mystical prayer, Hesychasm, and a great Marian theologian as we have seen.

In an age which saw a remarkable flowering of Catholic theology, universal in Europe, notably biblical in the United States, Orthodox theologians were not to be overlooked. That is one factor, not the last in the vitality of their Church. Since their Church was represented at the Second Vatican Council, as Observers, and since this Council was summoned in the cause of Christian unity, and as we have seen the Decree on Ecumenism spoke words of praise about the Orthodox, the Catholic faithful are encouraged to welcome evident signs of renewal and expansion in the great sister Church. Here, as everywhere, the truth shall set us free. We should be impressed by the emergence, in many countries of strong, wise leaders. Some particular factors are noteworthy.

XI

Syndesmos, the world association of Orthodox youth, makes a valuable contribution to Church life, stirring valid hope for the future. The meetings are held in widely differing centers and attendance and enthusiasm leave nothing to be desired. Another movement of promise is the Orthodox Congresses of Western Europe. The ninth was held in Saint-Laurent-sur-Sevre (Vendee) from Novembert 1 to November 3 , 1996; they are held every three years. The theme was "Questions of Today: Orthodox Approaches."

The dimensions and program of this congress indicate what has been said about the upsurge of Orthodoxy. There were about 700 participants from thirteen different countries. The opening discourse was from Metropolitan Jeremie, who read a message from the Ecumenical Patriarch, Bartholomew I "of Blessing, cordial greeting, warm and sincere wishes." Many Orthodox bishops of Europe send messages of support and blessing, as from the Catholic bishop of the diocese, Mgr. Francois Garnier of Lucon, who was present for part of the congress. The speakers, who included the outstanding theologian, Olivier Clement, addressed the problems of the hour with frankness. This is one of the laudable aspects of contemporary Orthodoxy.

The Orthodox Church benefits also by highly qualified presentation in the media. It is served in different countries by reviews or periodicals which are informative and well-edited. As an example, there is in France a thoughtful review, *Contacts*, and an excellent magazine, *Service Orthodoxe de Presse,*[20] carrying news, comment and important documents. I have found it invaluable in preparing the present book. The Patriarch, as we shall see, gives a very good example in dealing with the media; he has given several press conferences. More meaningful is the manifestation of Orthodox unity in the Episcopal assemblies which he has called, from 1990 on.

But is there not, at this very moment, a critical problem in Orthodox Roman Catholic relations? We have news of the cancellation, at the last minute, of a projected encounter in Austria between the Russian Patriarch, Alexei II and John Paul II; it was to have taken place before the ecumenical meeting in Graz. Still more saddening is the cancellation for the first time in twenty years of the annual delegation from the Ecumenical Patriarch to the Pope for the Feast of Saints Peter and Paul, June 29, 1997. As we shall see, the Patriarch himself made the visit in 1995. We await full information on these happenings.

We shall see that there is so much of a positive nature to record in regard to Orthodox Roman Catholic relations, all following on the initiative taken by Athenagoras, which we have noted. There is progress to relate on the theological level through the work of the

---

[20] I note in the U.S. *The Orthodox Church* and in Germany *Orthodoxes Forum.*

joint Orthodox Roman Catholic Commission. There has been progress likewise until now in the area of Church government. We must hope that the power of the Holy Spirit will enable all of us to overcome this obstacle on the path towards unity.

Chapter 2

Biographical Outline - Bartholomew I

I

The future patriarch was born on February 29, 1950 on the island of Imbros in Turkey, situated in the Aegean Sea, near the Dardanelles. In Baptism he was given the name Dimitrios by his parents, Christos and Maropi Archondonis. The island was at the time Greek Orthodox. His native village was named for two saints who bore the name Theodore. The capital of the island was Panaghia, the All-holy, an Orthodox title for Our Lady. Christos was proprietor of the village cafe, sometimes a barber, a man strict and exacting in behavior. He had four children, one daughter and three sons, Dimitrios the second. All have left their homeland, for the vicissitudes of politics have changed the island population from Greek to Turkish. Dimitrios helped in the cafe, as he would later during holidays. He would also recite poems for the customers; his interest in poetry, in art, is lifelong.

Dimitrios began his studies in the local primary school. He became involved with Church life. The village pastor, Father Asterios, was obliged to celebrate in places outside the village. He needed a companion and found one in Dimitrios. He would take care of the altar, and as a solo replace the absent choir.

What did the future hold? What could his primary studies in the island promise? Here we meet an important personality in the life of the future patriarch, Metropolitan Meliton. He was then Archbishop of Imbros and Tenedos, a prelate of quite remarkable quality. He knew all his faithful, including the Archondonis family. He saw the potential of Dimitrios, and, at his expense, sent him for further education to Istanbul. When, soon after, he set up a secondary school in Imbros, he invited Dimitrios to return. For three years the boy went five kilometers on foot to Pahaghia, returned in the evening. When his footwear gave out, the Metropolitan replaced them.

The next phase in his life was preparatory to his entry to the priesthood. He studied in the Orthodox seminary of Halki, an island in the sea of Marmara. The seminary was still functioning; it would be closed by the Turkish authorities in 1971. There, as I learned from a classmate of his now on the ministry in the United States, he was accepted by all as the brightest of the group. He has kept from those days a copybook in which he and his best friends, transcribed their favorite poems, all from the great poets of modern Greece. He did not neglect theology, for in 1961 he obtained his Licentiate with distinction. That year, on August 13, he was ordained deacon by Metropolitan Meliton; he was given the name Bartholomaios, Bartholomew, the name of one of the Apostles.

The future patriarch fulfilled his duty to the State as well as to the Church; from 1961 to 1963 he did his military service in the Turkish army at Gallipoli; this he completed with the rank of reserve officer. To look for a parallel to this experience in the life of a priest one must turn to France, where future priests are not exempt from military service. I have studied under a Dominican priest, in the University of Fribourg, a well-known writer in his day on spiritual subjects, Fr. Benoit Lavaud, who had been a captain in the French Army in the First World War. One of my colleagues in the Holy Ghost Congregation, Père Catlin, was a colonel in the French army in the Second World War; a French Carmelite father, Louis Thierry d'Argerlieu, was Admiral in Chief of the Free French Navy, a personal friend of De Gaulle, who obtained papal permission to retain him as Governor of Indo-China and Grand Chancelier of L'Ordre de la Liberation.

II

At this time, the mighty personality already mentioned, Athenagoras I, entered Bartholomew's life. The young student, who would one day be his successor, was brought to his notice favorably by his close associate, Metropolitan Meliton. The patriarch awarded the young student a bursary which would enable him to pursue his studies abroad.

Where would he go? Thinking of Orthodox unity and a unified canonical legal system as an important means to achieving it, he sought advice on the most suitable academic centers available to him. Rome and Munich were recommended. He went first to Rome, enrolled in the Pontifical Oriental Institute, attached to the Gregorian University. As Pope John Paul II remarked not long ago during a visit to the Institute, it had been founded in 1917 by Benedict XV, in the hope that one day Catholic and Orthodox students would there work side by side.

Bartholomew had a late start in his first year. Visa formalities delayed his arrival until December. He had an immediate setback on learning that the courses were given in Latin, of which he did not know a word. Despite the initial dismay, he set to work on the language and two months later passed his first examinations. French he would master also during his stay in Rome, as he was welcomed to the *Séminaire Francais*, directed by the Holy Ghost Fathers. Here he made friends with future French bishops; his fellow students were the flower of the French clergy.

Athenagoras had publicly voiced support and sympathy for John XXIII when the Pope, on January 25, 1959, announced his intention to call a General Council of the Church. Now Bartholomew was in Rome during the Council sessions. John who had lived in Turkey, knew the Orthodox Church there and in Bulgaria, was dead, but Paul VI guaranteed continuity of policy. The young student was conscious of the fact that for the first time in centuries there was an Orthodox presence at the Council: Observers empowered to assist at the conciliar debates, meeting regularly with the Secretariat for Christian Unity, making friends with bishops and theological experts; they were not allowed to intervene in debates or to vote. They were amply supplied with conciliar documentation, and some of them were effective in lobbying.

III

One thing the Council achieved. It showed to the world the intellectual vitality of the Catholic Church. Internal problems had been resolved. Theologians recently distrusted or marginalized were now conciliar experts. John XXIII had timed the Council for a Golden Age in Catholic Theology. If the names of Rahner, Ratzinger, De Lubac, Congar, Chenu, Phillips, Laurentin, Balic, Courtney Murray and others did not stir the interest in the young Orthodox student that they aroused in his European fellow students, he could not have been indifferent to what so affected them.

One of the tutorial staff of the French Seminary where Bartholomew stayed was an important conciliar expert. Père Joseph Lécuyer was the leading theologian of the priesthood in the Catholic Church, secretary to the commission charged with the Council text on the Ministry and Life of Priests.

Bartholomew concluded his studies in Rome with a doctorate thesis on *The Codification of the Holy Canons and the Canonical Constitution of the Orthodox Church*. His thesis was published in 1970 by the Patriarchal Institute for Patristic Studies. His work shows an important sense of history, points the way to a Code which would rise above transitory elements. Those interested in comparative Church law may refer to the Code ordered by St. Pius X in 1904, promulgated in 1917 and that which now replaces it, ordered by John XXIII in 1959, promulgated by John Paul II in 1983.

Leaving Rome, Bartholomew betook himself to the Bossey Institute, an academic center dependent on the World Council of Churches. The director was Nikos Nissiotis, an outstanding Greek theologian. Here he was initiated into contemporary philosophy, existentialism and personalism. He went on to Munich, where he had the advantage of adding German to his already rich linguistic equipment. He returned to Istanbul in 1968; he was appointed Assistant Dean of the Theological School of Halki. His ordination to the priesthood took place on October 19, 1969. Soon after that, Athenagoras promoted him to the rank of Archimandrite.

The great patriarch died in 1972. As to his successor, there was an immediate problem. Meliton, who had worked closely with him, was the obvious choice. But the Turkish government, by the Treaty of Lausanne, which ended the Greco-Turkish war in 1923, had the right to exercise a veto. They did so against him. Eyes then turned on Dimitrios, Metropolitan of Imbros and Tenedos. He refused with tears. But he yielded to the pleading of those around him.

IV

Who was Dimitrios? He was born in 1914 in Constantinople and studied for the priesthood at Halki Theological School. Between his ordination as deacon in 1937, and as priest in 1942, he was occupied in ministry in Edessa, Greece and Perikio, Constantinople. In 1945 he went to Tehran, Iran to organize and direct the Orthodox community; he also taught classical Greek in the University of Tehran.

Back in Constantinople he served in the ministry in Ferikioi. In 1964 he was elected Bishop of Elaia and acted also as director of the Diocese of Tataoula. In February he was elected Metropolitan of Imbros and Tenedos; five months later, on July 16, 1972, the Holy Synod of the Ecumenical Patriarchate chose him as successor to Athenagoras.

Dimitrios I continued in the spirit of his predecessor. He welcomed John Paul II to the Phanar on November 29, 1979 and returned the visit to Rome in December, 1987. At the first meeting a most important decision was taken: to set up a joint commission of Orthodox and Catholic theologians to discuss questions of mutual interest, somewhat as does the Anglican Roman Catholic International Commission established by Paul VI and Archbishop Ramsey. One document issued by this Orthodox Catholic body was something of a landmark, the Balamand Declaration, June 1993.

Showing his commitment to an understanding with the Papacy, Dimitrios made another innovation: every year on the Feast of Saints Peter and Paul, a delegation left Istanbul with a message of formal greeting for the Pope, who replied in similar form. The Pope then sent a delegation to Istanbul for the Feast of St. Andrew, November 30; the same formalities were observed. High dignitaries are appointed on each side to manifest status.

Within his own Orthodox world, the Patriarch was much engaged with preparation for the forthcoming Great and Holy Council of the Church. To this end he convened the First, Second and Third Pan-Orthodox Councils; they met in the Orthodox Center of the Ecumenical Patriarchate in Chambesy, Switzerland. Dimitrios traveled to visit several religious authorities, and to most of the autocephalous Orthodox Churches.

From 1972 until the death of Dimitrios in 1991 the relationship between him and Bartholomew was increasingly close on the personal and official levels. The Patriarch, soon after his election, established the private Patriarchal Office and appointed the Archimandrite as director; he retained this position until his election as Geron Metropolitan in January, 1990. On December 18, 1973 he was elected Metropolitan of the ancient See of Philadelphia by the Holy Synod of the Ecumenical Patriarchate; he was consecrated the following Christmas by Dimitrios and members of the Holy Synod. In March 1974, he was elected a member of the Holy Synod to take the place of deceased Metropolitan Dorotheos of the Prince's Islands.

On the death of the Geron Metropolitan Meliton of Chalcedon, whom Bartholomew considered his spiritual father, he was himself elected unanimously his successor and his enthronement took place on January 14, 1990 amid widespread approval and enthusiasm.

The future Patriarch was the senior Metropolitan of the Holy Synod. This meant a constant call to serve on special commissions; it meant membership and the presidency of the Canonical Commission, the Commission on Inter-Christian Relations, the Commission on Inter-Orthodox Relations.

The problem of one increasingly involved with the institutional Church is to preserve freshness of mind and warmth of heart. Not all succeed in this, if one may understate. Bartholomew was helped in the task by his close relationship on a personal level with his immediate superior, Patriarch Dimitrios. He accompanied his beloved leader in his meetings with the Orthodox Patriarchs, and the heads of the Autocephalous and Autonomous Churches, as with the World Council of Churches. He was also with the Patriarch on official visits to the Pope of Rome, the Archbishop of Canterbury and the World Council of Churches. He went in a representative capacity to general assemblies of the World Council of Churches in Upsala, 1968, in Vancouver, 1983, and in Canberra, 1991. Since 1975, he has been a member of the WCC Commission of Faith and Order; and since 1991 an elected member of the Executive and Central Committees of the organization. In November 1990, he presided at the Preparatory Inter-Orthodox Commission at Chambesy, Geneva which dealt with the subject of the Orthodox diaspora. He has served as a member of delegations to the Turkish government, to Moscow, Sofia, and to Mount Athos.

On the level of academic or scholarly pursuits the future Patriarch was a founder member of "The Society of Canon Law of the Oriental Churches" which is based in Vienna, and was its vice president for several terms. He was a member of the bi-lateral commission which prepared and edited the *Tomas Agapis*, (Rome-Istanbul, 1971); this contains the official correspondence between the Vatican and the Phanar between 1958 and 1970. He has answered several calls to lecture in universities — Athens, Thessalonika, Louvain, Madrid, Vienna, Rome. He is an honorary doctor of the Divinity School of Athens University and of the Holy Cross Greek Orthodox School of Theology in Brookline, Massachusettes; he is a Fellow of the Orthodox Academy of Crete and an honorary member of the *Pro-Oriente* Institute in Vienna. In such a varied and demanding intellectual commitment, he has been helped by a linguistic talent; besides Greek he speaks Turkish, French, English, German, Italian and Latin. A congenial gracious manner goes along with unusual resources of spiritual and intellectual energy; he is approachable, available to all he can help, and profoundly charitable.

V

Dimitrios died in October, 1991. Bartholomew, by reason of his seniority, presided over the synod. In its name, he informed the government at Ankara of the death of Dimitrios, and as was the custom, communicated the list of those eligible to succeed him. After three weeks, the government let it be known that they had no objection to the candidates; the relief of tension caused some excitement. Bartholomew first insisted on dealing with current matters. In the afternoon, the synod met in the patriarchal Church of St. George and the election took place. Bartholomew was thought to be the likely successor to Dimitrios, with whom he had traveled much, acting as a speech-writer, learning, too, by experience the universal mission of Orthodoxy.

A close associate of a deceased religious ruler is not always chosen to succeed him. Cardinal Percale succeeded Pius XI, with whom he worked in close partnership; Cardinal Merry de Val did not succeed St. Pius X — perhaps the fact that he was not Italian counted. Before the secret vote for the new Patriarch three names were retained: Bartholomew of Chalcedon, Constantinos of Derka, and Calinikos of Lystra. Bartholomew was elected unanimously.

The choice was interpreted as the will to see continuity with the policy of openness to the other Churches. A Western reader cannot help evoking the significance of the passage from Chalcedon, a name rich in doctrinal Tradition since the Council of 451, when the assembled fathers accepted the teaching of the Pope of Rome, Leo the Great, to the primatial See of the East, which had its dignity as the "New Rome," second to the city established by the Ecumenical Council of 381, confirmed by that held in Chalcedon.

VI

Roman Catholic reaction to the election of Bartholomew was immediate and warm. Cardinal Edward I. Cassidy issued this statement: "The new Patriarch is already well-known in Rome, because he came here as head of the Ecumenical Patriarchate's delegation over the last three years for the Feast of Saints Peter and Paul. We can certainly hope to have the same good relations which have been established over the last thirteen years."

John Paul II sent this congratulatory message to Bartholomew: "The announcement of your election as Ecumenical Patriarch has brought me great joy. The bonds of fraternal affection which already unite us will doubtlessly facilitate our collaboration in view of the re-establishment of full communion between our Churches. I ardently hope that the theological dialogue whose opening I had the joy of announcing with your beloved predecessor, Dimitrios I, on the occasion of my memorable visit to the Phanar will continue. May the Lord grant Your Holiness an abundance of his light and strength in your new and difficult pastoral charge. I assure you of my prayer and all my fraternal charity." November 4, 1991.

Cardinal Cassidy sent this message: "In my own name and in the name of the whole Pontifical Council for Promoting Christian Unity, I would like to express the joy we felt upon hearing of your election as Ecumenical Patriarch. It is my fervent wish that the fruitful cooperation between our Churches begun by your venerable predecessors Athenagoras I and Dimitrios I may continue and deepen, and that the blessings of the Lord may descend in abundance upon you and your whole Church. Be assured of our respectful and fraternal good wishes." October 26, 1991

Cardinal Johannes Willebrands, President Emeritus of the Pontifical Council for Promoting Christian Unity, a pioneer in ecumenical dialogue, sent this message: "I am united with Your Holiness in prayer that the Lord may fill you with His grace in the high calling and office which He has entrusted to you in the service of His Church." October 23, 1991

Bartholomew sent two letters to the Pope: one to acknowledge his congratulatory message, the other on November 2, the day of his enthronement:

> To His Holiness the Pope of Ancient Rome, John Paul II, greetings in the Lord.

> Having ascended to the most holy Ecumenical Throne by God's will and boundless mercy, we have received with emotion and joy the congratulatory message sent for this occasion by Your Holiness, whom we deeply love and respect.

> This participation in our joy, and that of the Church, by means of your fervent prayers and supplication strengthens us in our dedication to the accomplishment of God's desire for our Holy Church.

> Therefore, expressing our warmest thanks for your gracious message, and wishing for Your Holiness good

health and many years of primatial ministry and obla-
tion, we conclude with an expression of deep love in
Christ and profound respect. From Your Holiness' beloved Brother in Christ, Bartholomew of Constantinople,
October 28, 1991.

The second letter:

To His Holiness the Pope of Ancient Rome, John
Paul II, greetings in the Lord.

In line with the custom that has been established in
recent years, according to which those who have been
elevated to the holy apostolic Ecumenical Throne an-
nounce the spiritual enthronement by God's choice also
to the venerable Heads of the Christian Churches and
Confessions with which our Holy Orthodox Church is
engaged in a dialogue of charity and truth, we joyfully
address a letter also to your beloved Holiness, announcing to you and to your venerable Church our election by
the ineffable will of God, and by unanimous canonical
vote of the venerated Metropolitans, and our elevation
to the most holy Ecumenical Throne.

Sending, therefore, by means of this letter, fraternal
greetings to Your Holiness, and expressing our great joy
for the evident advancement of relations of charity and
respect between this holy Throne and the other holy
Orthodox Churches, on one hand and the venerable
Roman Catholic Church on the other, and for the
progress of the theological dialogue between them, we
assure your Holiness that, following the example of our
most holy predecessors, we will also commit ourselves,
at all times and with all care and readiness, to work to
consolidate even more the fraternal bonds which exist
between our Churches.

Asking from the Lord an abundance of gifts and
graces, as well as His blessings on all the faithful of
your Church, and asking that health and long life might

be granted to your Holiness, so that you might continue your illustrious primatial ministry for the good of the whole world, we offer you a holy embrace and we conclude with an expression of fraternal love and great respect, from your Holiness; beloved Brother in Christ, Bartholomew of Constantinople, November 2, 1991.

VII

Within a few weeks of the enthronement of Bartholomew, John Paul II's delegation arrived for the Feast of St. Andrew. As it was the first of the annual exchanges, the messages from the Pope to the Patriarch and the latter's reply, merit study in full.

Message of John Paul II to His holiness Bartholomew I, Archbishop of Constantinople, Ecumenical Patriarch.

For the first time since you assumed responsibility for the Ecumenical Patriarchate I have the great joy of expressing the warm best wishes of the Church of Rome to your Holiness for the Feast of St. Andrew, the patron of the Ecumenical Patriarchate.

The solemn celebration of the brother of Peter, the patron of the Church of Rome, once again gives me the opportunity of publicly demonstrating the bonds of deep affection which the Holy Spirit has established between our Churches, by sending a delegation led by His Eminence Cardinal Edward Idris Cassidy, President of the Pontifical Council for promoting Christian Unity. The delegation conveys the best wishes of all Catholics and demonstrates my personal participation in your celebration. I am also sure of the cordial reception which it will receive from Your Holiness.

Your election to the first See of the Orthodox Church moves me to recall with you this statement of St. Paul 'All this has been done by God, who had reconciled us to himself through Christ and has given us the ministry of reconciliation...This makes us ambassadors for Christ' (2 Cor. 5:18, 20). May the Lord grant that we may exercise in ever greater unity the ministry of reconciliation and that we may make every effort to promote the gathering of all in unity!

How could I forget at this time Your Holiness' two great predecessors, Patriarchs Athenagoras and Dimitrios? They made a decisive contribution to bringing about the dialogue of charity, and later the theological dialogue between our Churches. They tirelessly struggled to establish closer and deeper bonds of unity between the Churches, always keeping before them the vision of that day, which they hoped would come soon, when we would again be gathered around the same altar to celebrate the one Eucharist of the Lord.

It is by continuing this happily begun dialogue that we will be able to overcome the new tensions which have arisen in Central and Eastern Europe. It is necessary to learn again how to live in freedom, mutual respect and charity.

Last June, as the representative of Patriarch Dimitrios I to the celebration of the Feast of Saints Peter and Paul here in Rome, Your Holiness rightly exhorted 'the heads of the holy Churches of God,' of the East and the West, to seize the favorable opportunity which God is offering them at this time to overcome their divisions and to help bring peace and reconciliation to the human family as it begins the Third Millennium.

When the disciples went to look for Jesus and found him in a desert place where he had gone to pray, he said: 'Let us move on to the neighboring villages so that I may proclaim the Good News there also. That is what I have come to do' (Mk. 1:38). In this way Jesus points out the task which belongs to His followers. But we know that the fruitfulness of this mission depends on our unity (cf.Jn 17:21). It is in unity together that we proclaim the Gospel in our modern societies. Let us take pains to respond to this appeal 'so that in all ways God may be glorified through Jesus Christ' (1 Pt. 4:11).

With these sentiments, and invoking the intercession of Saints Peter and Andrew, I assure you, dear
brother, of my feelings of profound fraternal charity.
From the Vatican, November 23, 1991, John Paul II.

Since the whole subject of this book is intended to interest and
inform Catholics I note that John Paul's message on the election of
Bartholomew and this letter sent for the first occurrence of the Feast
of St. Andrew were an innovation. This was the first time that a
Pope made such gestures to an Ecumenical Patriarch on his assumption of office. It sets the tone for all that will follow through
the subsequent years, the continuation of the annual visits of delegations to Constantinople and Rome. The visit of the Patriarch to
Rome in June 1995 will be a climax, but will not mark an end.

It is in this context also the reply of Bartholomew to the papal
message should be read.

Your Eminence Cardinal Edward Idris Cassidy, Dear
Fathers and Brothers.

Our most holy Church of Constantinople, the most
reverend brothers and concelebrants around us, and we,
personally, welcome today with great joy the honorable
Delegation of the Church of Rome of her eminently dear
to us Prinate, His Holiness Pope John Paul II, on the
occasion of the most venerable commemoration of Andrew, the First-called among the Apostles, the founder
and patron of our Church.

For all of us our joy is indeed great, because on this
propitious day and hour we see again among us beloved
brothers with whom for years we with sincerity have
been collaborating to promote not only the relationship
between our sister Churches, but also pan-Christian rapprochement in general and, through this means, peace
throughout the whole world.

Our humble selves, having often had, even until recently, the privilege to lead an analogous delegation of
the Church of Constantinople to the Elder Rome, wel-

come today with entirely special emotion the delegation headed by Your Eminence, beloved Cardinal Cassidy, since we meet for the first time under the new and even greater charge to which the ineffable will of the benevolent God has called us in ascending the most venerable Ecumenical Throne.

Precisely because of this, that is, because we have personally repeatedly experienced how sacred is the task at hand, which is repeated each year in the form of fraternal courtesy and ecclesiastical etiquette, we are in a position to appreciate it in all its importance.

To one who sees these yearly reciprocal official visits from the outside only, the whole content of the mission at hand is perhaps not evident; such a mission certainly does not exhaust itself by the official presence of each side attending the solemn Divine Liturgy of the other on its patronal feast, but extends itself to other silent but not less substantial dimensions of the meeting and collaboration on this occasion.

Thus each year a new sincere effort is undertaken to survey together, indeed from the highest ecclesiastical watch-tower, not only the bilateral relations and the responsibilities assumed each time by each side, but also the general situation between Roman Catholics and Orthodox throughout the world, since this is required by the ecclesiology professed on both sides according to which 'if one member suffers, all suffer together with it.' (cf. 1 Cor. 12: 26).

It is, however, well understood that, when the occasion presents itself, often matters of pan-Christian interest as well as issues related to the universal responsibility of the Church are examined together with the same ecclesiological sensitivity.

Moreover, it is no secret that, on the one hand, the purely theological approach to dogmatic differences and the 'theoretical' problems existing between our sister Churches have for the past ten years, been assigned to our official theological dialogue, whereas, on the other hand, the difficulties established in this official theological dialogue, or those which arise otherwise require that they be confronted each time pastorally, and in a practical manner through the competent ecclesiastical authorities. To this end, the yearly exchange of these blessed delegations is a considerable contribution.

Precisely in this spirit, most honorable brothers, we wish also during this most sacred moment to remind you and, through you, the beloved Primate of the Church of Rome, His Holiness Pope John Paul II, that the decennial work accomplished by our theological dialogue, something truly historic for pan-Christian matters in general, unfortunately not only risks being — indefinitely and with unknown outlooks — suspended, but perhaps even being halted entirely, which should not be, due to the inadmissible situation created by the Uniates in Eastern and Central Europe in their relationships with the local Orthodox Churches which constitute the ancient traditional dominant Christian faith in the region, towards which, understandably, greater respect and fraternal trust ought to be demonstrated.

Of course, the present moment is not the most appropriate to extend ourselves once more to the individual aspects of this paramount problem — something which one way or the other has been done in the discussions held between your honorable Delegation and our Synodical Commission — but we must in all fraternal sincerity stress at this first blessed meeting since we assume our humble Patriarchy, that just as we shall in no way spare fatigue and pain so that the praiseworthy task systematically undertaken during the past decennia of our reconciliation and possible reunion one day might be advanced in the manner most suitable to God, by the same measure we shall not cease to stigmatize, with fear of God and out of our most sacred duty, all pertinent illegitimate actions or breakings of faith, regardless of which side or position they might come from.

At any rate, today we are in the pleasant position to communicate as well to your Delegation our joy and that of the Holy Synod around us in the founding of a separate Orthodox Archdiocese of Italy, always under the immediate jurisdiction and dependence of our Ecumenical Throne, and this, of course, not for the sake of any proselytizing activity in the West, for such an intention is, as is known, entirely foreign to our Church and tradition — especially in these times in which the fraternal relations between us, due precisely to the theological dialogue in progress, must be shielded as the pupil of the eye — but for the same of caring for the multiple spiritual needs of the students or of other Orthodox faithful established in Italy.

The fact that we have chosen as first chief pastor of this newly-founded holy archdiocese the head of the Orthodox secretariat of the Dialogue in progress between us, His Eminence Spyridon, formerly Bishop of Apameia, clearly reveals, that through this new institution of our Church, we wish to sustain the reconciliation and collaboration pursued through the dialogue even more effectively. Thus we are certain that this first Orthodox Metropolitan of Italy, His Eminence Spyridon, will enjoy not only the indisposition and trust of the sister Roman Catholic Church in all things, but also the active assistance wherever it might be needed and wherever it is possible for the accomplishment of his difficult and truly delicate mission.

With such fraternal thoughts and with such perspectives, greeting once again your honorable Delegation, we ask of you to assure once again our most holy brother, John Paul II, who sent you, of our unaltered good intentions and sentiments. We fervently wish that this time, too, your blesses sojourn to our Church and City be enjoyable, according to God, and exceedingly constructive for is sacred aim. Amen.

Chapter 3

Ecclesiastical Office

Bartholomew I was solemnly enthroned on November 2, 1991. The event was marked by solemnity and the presence of important guests. It is especially memorable for the address given by the new Patriarch.[1] Taking as his text the word of one of his saintly predecessors, John Chrysostom, "Glory to God for all things," Bartholomew offered to his audience a lucid summary of the Orthodox ecclesiology, an affirmation of respect for the lawful government of his country, and a practical program of action based on his experience with Dimitrios. He did not lack attention to his distinguished guests; nor gratitude to those who had unanimously elected him.

On his conception of Orthodox ecclesiology: "Thus we assert straight-away that not only shall we follow the canonical order of our Orthodox Church, and especially respect in particular the revered tradition and the experience of the great Church of Christ, but what is more, by lived holy experience of the irreplaceable value of the conciliar spirit through which the Holy Spirit speaks in the Church, we shall walk in the light of the church and solely without leaving its proper framework and its canonical action, maintaining harmony with our revered brethren and concelebrants in Christ, in the way of service to the Church. But when we call to mind this capital point, our conviction and intention are in no way

---

[1] SP., November, 1991.

limited to what interests our holy Church of Constantinople but extends to all that is of concern to the entirety of the Orthodox Church in the whole world."[2]

Church State relations are sensitive in Istanbul. The Orthodox seminary where Bartholomew had studied was shut down by the government; he hopes that it will be reopened. This situation explains his clear statement of policy: "On this solemn occasion when before God and mankind we accept the responsibility of ecumenical watchman we wish to affirm that we assume our responsibilities under the protection of the constitution and laws of the Republic of Turkey. Preserving the centuries old tradition of the patriarchs after the fall of Constantinople, we shall remain a faithful citizen and subject to the law of our country, as are the spiritual children of the Church; we shall serve God and follow in all integrity and sincerity the commandment of the Lord to give to Caesar what belongs to Caesar (Mt. 22:21). In this regard we think it our duty to state clearly that the Ecumenical Patriarchate exists as a purely spiritual institution, a symbol of reconciliation and an unarmed force. In its application of the principles of the holy Orthodox faith, in the support which it gives to other Orthodox jurisdictions, the Ecumenical Patriarchate remains detached from every political aim, and keeps apart from 'the deceitful arrogance of the secular power.'"

The Patriarch went on to thank the Greek government, represented by its head, Constantin Mitsotakis, to bless the "pious Orthodox Greek people represented by an official parliamentary delegation"; he also thanked the president of the United States who sent an official delegation.

After sending greetings to all his people and their pastoral rulers Bartholomew registered an important decision: "We shall convene meetings of all the bishops of the Ecumenical Patriarchate at its seat, to be mutually informed and strengthened and with a view to elaborating common projects."

The reader knows the importance of monasticism in the Orthodox Church. He or she will have striking evidence of it in the

---

[2] Texts here quoted from *Information Service*, issued by The Pontifical Council for Promoting Christian Unity, No. 81, 1991.

words spoken by Bartholomew in his enthronement address; one cannot imagine any such pronouncement from a Pope or prelate in the Latin Church on a similar occasion.

"We speak in a very particular way from this ecumenical Throne to the revered and beloved fathers of the desert, who give themselves to the ascetical life on Mount Athos. We affirm that it is neither conceivable or possible, not for one single moment, that Mount Athos could exist, that the venerable monastic Orthodox tradition could be maintained and could blossom, apart from its sacred links with the Mother Church. We therefore think it is our duty to do everything for the preservation, the prosperity, the blossoming, the protection and the influence of the Holy Mountain, while respecting the canonical order of the Orthodox Church and the spirit of its hierarchical structure. We ask from our fathers exactly what we demand of ourselves: the active practice of the two fundamental monastic virtues, namely humility and obedience to the Church in the fear of God and in total fidelity to their monastic vows.

We have nothing more to add in speaking to the historic monastery of the Beloved Disciple at Patmos and to the other monastic centers attached to this Throne, save that we embrace them with affection, esteem and interest not any less great."

Mount Athos is unique as a monastic settlement in the East, indeed in the world. The incoming Patriarch was aware of tension between the twenty monasteries and his predecessor over the latter's policy in regard to the Papacy. Hence, his words of conciliation.

Bartholomew I addressed his greetings by name to all his fellow Patriarchs; he did likewise to the other churches with which the Orthodox have been in dialogue. A Catholic writer may single out what he said about the Pope and the World Council of Churches.

On the Pope: "From this sacred enclosure we greet likewise His Holiness the Pope of the first Rome, with whom we are in communion of love. We assure him that one of our most serious concerns will be the realization of the sacred vision of our recent predecessors, Athenagoras and Dimitrios, so that the ways of the Lord will be accomplished on earth for his holy Church, in the reunion of all those who believe in him, by means of a dialogue in truth. We shall do all in our power to make progress in this direction in the fear of God, in sincerity, honesty and prudence. We are convinced that our brother in the West will exhaust the numerous possibilities at his disposal and will cooperate with us in view of this holy and sacred objective."

On the World Council of Churches: "From this sacred seat we address our greeting in Christ in a very special way to the World Council of Churches, to the president of the central committee here present among us, to the general secretary, to his invaluable team, as well as to all the member Churches. We have had the joy, through many years and in different offices, of collaborating and keeping up the struggle side by side with those who work within the Council, of sharing our common anxieties on the quest for and building up of Christian unity, as well as in the attitude and witness of Christians before the contemporary problems of humankind. We consider the Council as an important expression of the ecumenical movement and an implementation of the ecumenical spirit.

"The Ecumenical Patriarchate, which is one of the founder members of the Council, will in no way lessen its interest in the proper progress of the initiatives taken by this Council and it will take care that there is no departure from the first principles of its mission: the service of Christian unity. That is the position of all the Churches, as has been proved by our common action at Canberra and Chambesy."

Bartholomew also sent greetings to the Council of European Churches of which the Ecumenical Patriarchate is a member. He promised to "knit good relations with the principal non-Christian religions, so as to collaborate in a practical way in safeguarding and maintaining the spiritual and moral values of true civilization and the rejection of all forces which are negative and lethal to the human person."

Three further engagements made by the Patriarch reveal his true Christ-like magnanimity. To those beyond all religious commitment he spoke thus: "If need be we shall not refuse dialogue even with those who are ignorant of, reject or even insult God. Rather, we shall convey to them, precisely to them, the witness of Christ's love, he who left the ninety sheep to seek the only one lost, for Christ was crucified for this one (Mt. 18:12).

"The great Church of Christ, called from on high and from the beginning to be a Church of evangelization cannot renege on this.

It cannot not evangelize and not be continually re-evangelized; 'And woe to me if I do not preach the Gospel'" (1 Cor. 9:16).

Next hear the words spoken for youth — here he joins in thought Pope John Paul II, who inaugurated the World Youth Day and has traveled to different countries and continents to preside over the ceremonies: "We address very specially and wholeheartedly our fatherly greetings and our patriarchal blessing to youth, which not only makes our future but also our present with its dynamism, this present without which there could not be a future. Our Mother the Church expresses through me her infinite and sincere sympathy towards all the problems of youth today across the world; their problems are ours."

A third preoccupation of the Patriarch was the state of theological studies: "During the period of our humble patriarchal service we shall, in no way, neglect theological studies, not only because this is the tradition of our Church, but also because our personal conviction is therein involved. We shall watch over their development so that they may be shown to be effective in their way of interpreting Orthodox tradition in the context of our time. The Ecumenical Patriarchate must acquire the proper means to develop Orthodox theology and encourage research. In this context we shall continue our approaches to the State authorities to obtain permission to reopen the Theological School of Halki, which was forced to interrupt its activities twenty years ago. In addition the publication of a church and official theological review, where its theological thought and its experience of the unbroken tradition will be set forth; will remain for your humble servant a principal concern, and it will retain his very particular interest."

The Patriarch with this magnificent proclamation of doctrinal and ecclesial policy went on to enunciate certain practical decisions.

"Besides it is our intention:

to honor the memory of our holy predecessors, the Patriarchs of Constantinople, as their successor, called to pursue their struggle, by the celebration of the Divine Liturgy in the venerable patriarchal church, beginning with Paul the Confessor, this Wednesday, sixth day of the month;

to reinforce the observance of liturgical practices proper to the Great Church. Promotion of liturgical life in conformity with the Typikon of our Church will be the object of our particular concern, because it is the center of our life and our existence as Christians;

to publish annually the calendar of the Ecumenical Patriarchate;

to reinforce and use fully the patriarchal Institute of patristic studies in Thessalonika, the Orthodox center of the Ecumenical Patriarchate at Chambesy, the patriarchal monastery of St. Anastasios Pharmakolytria in Chalcidia and the Orthodox Academy in Crete;

to consecrate during the Holy Week of this year a new quantity of Holy Chrism, the supply contained in the patriarchal reserve having much decreased;

to reinforce and modernize the infrastructures of the Patriarchate so that work may be less tiring and more productive."

Chapter 4

Pope and Patriarch

I

It is tempting to compare the two Christian leaders in the tenth decade of the century, to look for points of resemblance despite obvious differences. The first difference is of age; John Paul II is twenty years older than Bartholomew. He is from a Christian Slav culture, while the Patriarch has a cultural background that is Greek, but in a minority situation in a Muslim country, Turkey. The Polish Catholics were always a majority, but in Karol Wojtyla's formative years this majority was held down by an occupying force. The future Patriarch could complete his studies in the School of Theology in Halki, which had not yet been closed. The future Pope was driven out of his University at Cracow, which was closed down, and he worked first in a stone quarry, then in the Solway firm in Cracow. His priestly studies were begun in an underground seminary, kept in existence by a man who influenced him powerfully, Adam later Cardinal, Sapieha, archbishop of the city.

Sapieha it was who sent him to Rome to study at the Angelico Dominican University, where he would prepare his doctorate thesis on *Faith in the Writings of St. John of the Cross*. As we have seen, the protective shadow of a great prelate, Athenagoras, was about Bartholomew; he guided him to Rome also, to the Jesuit University, the Pontifical Oriental Institute, where he specialized in law. Bartholomew was not in a Greek but a French College; Karol Wojtyla was not in a Polish but a Belgian College — it took some time after the war to restore the Polish house.

Intellectually Karol added to his study of a Catholic doctor of mysticism something apparently at the other end of the spectrum, phenomenology. He specialized in Max Scheler and published some fifty important essays in this whole philosophical domain, notably *The Acting Person*. He would as Pope beatify another specialist in this branch of philosophy, Edith Stein, favorite pupil of Edmond Huserl, founder; in the Carmelite Order she was Sister Benedicta of the Cross. The way is now open for her canonization.

Both Pope and Patriarch travel much, the Pope more extensively for obvious reasons. That is the visible face of a sincere heartfelt yearning for unity and a resolve to do everything possible to see it come to pass.

On the Pope's side, the quest for unity with the Orthodox has meant personal study of Orthodox theology and history, some evidence for which we have seen. It has meant fidelity to the annual visits from the Vatican to the Phanar; and welcome to those from Constantinople who came to Rome: visits in each case by delegations, save on two occasions, one of which we shall study. The Patriarch had likewise been true to the example of his predecessor, Dimitrios. He has had to face opposition from within his own Orthodox world. When a journalist of *Le Figaro* pointed this out to him he replied, "Unity is not a luxury, it is a duty."

He is respectful and warm-hearted towards John Paul II, but quite frank in his statement of the obstacle to be overcome, following a rule he enunciated in a message to the Pope, "Let us seek the truth in charity."

II

Difficulties in the past centered on the *Filioque*, that is the addition of this word to the Creed, *qui ex Patre Filioque procedit* (who proceeds from the Father and the Son), on the use of unleavened bread for the Eucharist in the Latin Church, on the Epiclesis, that is the invocation of the Holy Spirit at the Consecration in the Eucharistic celebration, and on the primacy of the Bishop of Rome as defined by the First Vatican Council and renewed by Vatican II.

Only the last difficulty now remains. The present Pope had shown his readiness to recite the Creed without the *Filioque*; the Orthodox do not any longer make an issue of the unleavened bread; the Eucharistic Prayers in use in the Catholic Church since the reforms following Vatican II have the Epiclesis, Eucharistic Prayer I, the old Roman Canon implicitly, Eucharistic Prayers II, III and IV explicitly.

The Primacy of the Roman Pontiff remains the sole obstacle to full unity between Catholics and Orthodox. We have seen what the Patriarch said in his enthronement address. Speaking to the Swiss bishops in Zurich on December 14, 1995 he made a plea that the conciliar system be kept unchanged. He also said that nowhere in the New Testament could it be seen that Peter was given authority over the other Apostles.[1]

The Second Vatican Council taught the doctrine of episcopal collegiality: "Just as, in accordance with the Lord's decree, St. Peter and the rest of the Apostles constitute a unique apostolic college, so in like fashion the Roman Pontiff, Peter's successor, and the bishops the successors of the Apostles, are related with and united to one another."[2]

That would meet Bartholomew's wish. But in the same Constitution on the Church it is followed by this statement: "The college or body of bishops has for all that no authority unless united with the Roman Pontiff, Peter's successor, as its head whose primatial authority, let it be added, over all, whether pastors or faithful, remains in its integrity. For the Roman Pontiff, by reason of his office as Vicar of Christ, namely and as pastor of the whole Church, a power which he can always exercise unhindered."[3]

III

Bartholomew's opinion of this dogmatic position was expressed with characteristic honesty. By a strange irony it appeared in a Polish weekly, *Tygodnik Powsechny*, which appears in Cracow where John Paul was archbishop; the editor, Jerzy Turowicz, was a friend of his and it is believed that he occasionally supplied him with copy unsigned. The Ecumenical Patriarch was replying to questions put to him about papal primacy. "It is a fact," he said, "that the papal

---

[1] SP., February, 1996.

[2] Construction on the Church, 22.

[3] Ibid.

office has become the biggest obstacle and greatest threat to Christian unity as it has developed in the Western Church especially after two great schisms. ...This has been publicly recognized and confirmed not only under the current Pope John Paul II, but also even in a more dramatic way under Popes Paul VI and John XXIII." He said that the office and service of the Bishop of Rome had become "a real problem for inter-Church relationship" already in the early Christian centuries and the obstacles had increased after the proclamation of papal infallibility by the First Vatican Council in 1870. He thought that the recent statements of John XXIII and Paul VI, and the Encyclical of John Paul II, *Ut Unum Sint* would "undoubtedly have been accepted with gratitude" by all other denominations if the Catholic Church had shown readiness to consider the office of Pope in the context of the Pentarchy, the first millennium doctrine which vested Church authority with the patriarchs of Rome, Constantinople, Alexandria, Antioch and Jerusalem.[4]

Acute consciousness of this problem has not deflected the Patriarch from the arduous course towards unity on which he has entered. This will be evident in the following pages.

IV

The Pope, on his side, has strained every effort to reach an understanding with the Orthodox. We have seen how he spoke of them in the Letter *Orientale Lumen*. Three weeks later in the Encyclical Letter *Ut Unum Sint*, he returned to the theme. He reminds his readers of the directive given by Vatican II to those "who plan to devote themselves to the work of restoring the full communion that is desired between the Eastern Churches and the Catholic Church, to give due consideration to these special aspects of the origin and growth of the Churches of the East, and to the character of the relations obtained between them and the Roman See before the separation, and to form for themselves a correct evaluation of facts."[5]

The Pope then tells again the epoch-making events which marked the Patriarchate of Athenagoras and the pontificate of Paul VI. He continues: "Following the death of Pope Paul VI and the

---

[4] Cf., *The Tablet*, July 6, 1996.
[5] CTS edition.

brief pontificate of Pope John I, when the ministry of Bishop of Rome was entrusted to me, I considered it one of the first duties of my pontificate to renew personal contact with the Ecumenical Patriarch Dimitrios I, who had meanwhile succeeded Patriarch Athenagoras in the See of Constantinople. During my visit to the Phanar on November 29, 1979, the Patriarch and I were able to decide to begin theological dialogue between, and all the Orthodox Churches in canonical communion with the See of Constantinople. In this regard it would seem important to add that at that time preparations were already under way for the convocation of the future Council of the Orthodox Churches. The quest for harmony between them contributes to the life and vitality of these sister Churches; this is also significant in view of the role they are called to play in the path towards unity. The Ecumenical Patriarch decided to repay my visit, and in December 1987, I had the joy of welcoming him to Rome with deep affection and with the solemnity due to him."

Recalling the celebration of the eleventh centenary of Saints Cyril and Methodius, whom he had named, with St. Benedict, patrons of Europe, John Paul II reminds us that they came "from the background of the Byzantine Church of their day, at a time when the latter was in communion with Rome." The Pope had also joined in the Millennium of Rus, in 1988, emphasizing that "the Baptism conferred on Saint Vladimir in Kiev was a key event in the evangelization of the world. The Slav peoples and those beyond the Urals as far as Alaska owe their faith to this."

"In this perspective," writes the Pope, "an expression which I have frequently employed finds its deepest meaning: the Church must breathe with her two lungs! In the first Millennium of the history of Christianity, this expression refers primarily to the relationship between Byzantium and Rome. From the time of the Baptism of Rus it came to have an even wider application: evangelization spread to a much vaster area, so that now it includes the entire Church."[6]

V

he reader is advised to read the full development of the Pope's thought, which includes the warrant from Pope Paul VI of the title

---

[6] Ibid.

"Sister Churches," and the Pope's firm statement of purpose: "In view of all this, the Catholic Church desires nothing less than full communion between East and West."

But what of the primacy of Rome, the "stumbling-block"? John Paul I was a participant in the Second Vatican Council which renewed the teaching of the First Vatican Council on the subject. In the present Encyclical he sets the doctrine in the context of communion. He then wrote these lines: "As Bishop of Rome I am fully aware, as I have reaffirmed in the present Encyclical Letter, that Christ ardently desires the full and visible communion of all those Communities in which, by virtue of God's faithfulness, his Spirit dwells." Asserting in the first person his responsibility, he wishes to heed the request to exercise the primacy in a way "which, while in no way renouncing what is essential to its mission, is nonetheless open to a new situation."

Already in his meeting with Dimitrios I, John Paul II had spoken thus: "I insistently pray the Holy Spirit to shine His light upon us, enlightening all the Pastors and theologians of our Churches that we may seek, together of course, the forms in which this ministry may accomplish a service of love recognized by all concerned." Now in the Encyclical he writes thus: "This is an immense task, which we cannot refuse and which I cannot carry out by myself. Could not the real but imperfect communion existing between us persuade Church leaders and their theologians to engage with me in a patient and fraternal dialogue on this subject, a dialogue in which leaving useless controversies behind, we could listen to one another, keeping before us the will of Christ for His Church and allowing ourselves to be deeply moved by His plea 'that they all be one...so that the world may believe that You have sent Me.'" (Jn. 17:21)[7]

No Pope had written anything like this. The writer has so much to win him sympathy from the Orthodox. He is the Pope of the Holy Spirit, author of a volume of teaching on this subject which surpasses all that all his predecessors taken collectively have taught on the Paraclete. He is the Pope of the Theotokos, beloved of the Orthodox. And, he has a holy obsession with the Church at the present time.

---

[7] Ibid.

Chapter 5

The Modern World

Followers of Jesus Christ, who believe that He is the Savior of humankind, have to contend with many opponents. There are those who openly persecute them, with different forms of pressure, even torture. These often just put them to death. There are those who seek to marginalize them, to set a dividing line between religion and the serious problems of our people. "Put religion back into the sacristy" might be their slogan. They would make no obstacle to the practice of religion provided it was not seen to have a bearing on their political, social or economic plans.

Such an experiment was tried in France at the beginning of the century, when *l'ecole laique* was proposed as the answer. It was officially non-denominational. In practice it often turned out to be a hot-bed of anti-clericalism, something which is explanable in terms of French history. This need not detain us.

The problem remained. There were those who asked just what was the relation between the Church and the world of our time, a world torn with agonizing problems. In the first session of the Second Vatican Council, two of the participants, Cardinal Montini (later Pope Paul VI) and Cardinal Suenens, proposed that the Council must face this challenge. Their idea was accepted and the result was the Pastoral Constitution on the Church in the Modern World. Both Cardinals knew that Pius XII in his writings and addresses had covered a vast spectrum.

The Catholic Church has an international membership of over eight hundred million. This would give widespread relevance to any such pronouncement. What of the Orthodox Church with a membership of altogether less than this? The answer is in ancient roots, in the intrinsic value of their creed, in their willingness to bear witness even in the face of martyrdom.

Bartholomew I, as his enthronement address made clear, is determined to speak to the modern world as it exists, to manifest the relevance of the Orthodox faith and tradition to the problems of our time. Some extracts from his public pronouncements which follow will show how accurate is his discernment of these problems of our time. He knows that this generation of young people are "the AIDS generation." He, like his predecessor, Dimitrios I, sees the reality of the massive threat to our environment by all that is being done at the present time. John Paul II has spoken of this subject over twenty times so it is not a surprise that when they met and made a common declaration they would include this concern in what they agreed upon.

The Patriarch's commitment to the World Council of Churches is plenary. As we shall see, essential reading is the memorandum sent from the patriarchate on the future of WCC.[1] Enlightening reading, too, is the text of Bartholomew's address to the European parliament. On a different level and of universal import is the Patriarch's decision to commemorate the nineteenth centenary of the Apocalypse composed on the island of Patmos by St. John.

Bartholomew I has believed in making personal contact with the other patriarchates, with the Orthodox not in communion with Constantinople and with the other Christian Churches or communions. His visit to Rome calls for separate reflection. Worthy of attention is his contact with the Anglican Church and altogether special were his days spent with the Catholics of France, that is with their hierarchy. Like all the great ones of history, Bartholomew has registered a number of "firsts"; he has had the intuition and the courage to innovate, again and again. In such innovation, history tells us, the enduring effect is commensurate with the vision of the one who is at the origin.

---

[1] Cf., Appendix III.

Chapter 6

Europe

On April 19, 1994, *Le Figaro*, a well-known Paris daily, published an interview with Bartholomew I. Among the questions he was asked was this: "After the fall of communist totalitarianism what influence does Orthodoxy wish to exercise in Europe today?" His reply: "The fall of communist totalitarianism gives Orthodoxy the possibility of restoring its people's confidence, faith and hope. For the first time in many years the whole Orthodox world can, in its diversity, bear witness to its vocation or communion, solidarity, and brotherhood. More particularly, in the context of the greater Europe now being built, peoples of Orthodox culture, through their spiritual inheritance, can contribute to make the scale of values ruling the world more just and more human. The role of the Ecumenical Patriarch of Constantinople, who has the mission of watching over the universal character of Orthodoxy and of manifesting its unity, is to provide the necessary impulse towards this end."

On the same day, Bartholomew I spoke to the European Parliament in Strasbourg. He was answering an invitation to do so from M.Egon Klepsch, the president. Only heads of state are given this honor. When the Pope spoke to the assembly, he was doing so as head of the Catholic Church and of the Vatican City State. The vision embodied in a united Europe found a sympathetic response in the Orthodox Church: "The unity of Europe to which you are devoting your powers, as representing the will of the peoples who elected you, is for us a familiar task. We serve a tradition of seventeen centuries, made up of preoccupations and combats for the salvation and unity of European civilization. We, the ancient patriarchate of New Rome, Constantinople, as our namesake, this other European axis, Old Rome, have not had the happiness of making this unity visible. For this we feel deep sadness. Nevertheless, we continue and singularly in a common approach, to bear our first witness: political unity, cut off from civilization, that is from the basic meaning of human relations, cannot attain the realization of European unity. The unity for which the peoples of Europe yearn, cannot come about, save as unity in communion in regard to a common meaning of life and a unique purpose in human relations."[1]

The Patriarch pointed to the Orthodox Church as an inspiration, possibly a model for European unity, rebutting the criticism made of the Orthodox in ex-Yugoslavia: "It is striking that the organization of the Christian Orthodox Church — with its high decree of administrative autonomy and the local authority of bishops, patriarchs and autocephalous Churches, to which is added at the same time, Eucharistic unity in the faith — could serve as a prototype of what is now made institutional by the European union as the principle of subsidiarity this being the most efficacious method of expressing its powers. In spite of the profound upheavals known to European history, Old Rome and New Rome are still regarded as axes of reference and unity for medieval civilization."

"We know" the Patriarch said with reference to ex-Yugoslavia, "that presently many of you load on our person and on the Catholic Orthodox Church which we serve as first in rank, the tragic reality of an abominable war actually going on, and in which the Orthodox populations of Europe are involved, fighting with neighboring heterodox peoples and those of other religions. The Ecumenical Patriarchate and the Orthodox Church in general respect national traditions and the susceptibilities of peoples. Nevertheless we condemn — and that in the clearest manner — all forms of fanaticism, all violation of law, all violence, from whatever they come. We persist, unshakably in our belief in the necessity of free and pacific

---

[1] SP., Juillet-Aout, 1994; Jacques Delors' population estimate for the Orthodox, if it was meant worldwide, would need to be raised to 300 at least.

relations between men, in the need for mutual respect and peaceful coexistence between peoples, as we emphasized in the very recent Bosphorus Declaration, published at the time of the congress *For Peace and Tolerance*, which we called on our own initiative."

Bartholomew mentioned grave and pressing problems to which his listeners should address their attention: "Measures for the protection of the weak and of minorities, whatever they are; let freedom of thought and expression be guaranteed, as free movement of persons and their settlement where natural, spiritual and social needs make this imperative for them. And more especially it is your task to create conditions which will allow the promotion of cooperation and unity between peoples and persons, the call to lessen and, still more, to suppress the inequality noticeable between the rich, undeveloped world and the under-developed world."

This inequality, the Patriarch thought, portends danger for the future of humanity. But united Europe, he thought, should not be seen in terms of merely "uniform economic development or of a political program of common defense." By the nature of things this vision similarly calls for a common social policy based on pacific, fruitful cooperation between the European peoples. the imperative is in the cultural order. It is an imperative about the meaning in the relations between persons and in mutual relations between national traditions.

The Patriarch had penetrating things to say about the way in which without a true hierarchy of values the economy assumes a kind of autonomy. He spoke of the burden of unemployment and, as we shall see again, of a theme which is at the center of his thinking, ecology. He promised the full cooperation of the Orthodox Church to any program, on a pan-European scale, designed to deal with these challenges. he recalled an interesting event, luminous on how God allows his children to profit by their "weakness:" In 1920 the Ecumenical Patriarchate took the initiative of a universal encyclical addressed to all the Christian churches and communions inviting them to a kind of "League of Churches" like the League of Nations, which was then the forerunner of the present day Organization of United Nations. From this initiative and with the contribution of the Protestant confessions, the World Council of Churches was born. "...The Ecumenical Patriarchate," he reminded his listeners, "had instituted, in union with the other sister Orthodox Churches, theological dialogue with the ancient Churches of the East as with the Roman Catholic Church, the Church of the Old Catholics, the Anglican Church, the Lutheran Church, and the Churches which came from the (Calvinist) Reform." He recalled the encounters between his predecessors and the Popes.

The Patriarch's final words merit special consideration:

> Your delicate invitation has allowed us to profit with you of this brief but precious time of personal communion. We feel responsibility of a weight difficult to carry; we have to sum up, in our poor words, the history and experience of an institution of seventeen centuries, which served as an axis of unity for the civilization of Europe. We have the honor to take on the succession of the word in the Ecumenical Patriarchate, New Rome, Constantinople following the word of St. John Chrysostom, Gregory the Theologian, Photius the Great, of a pleiad of patriarchs of Constantinople, who were giants, not only as regards ecclesiastical history, but European history.

> Historical crises have unsettled the world from top to bottom. We ask you to accept our presence here as a reminder: a reminder that we exist; that we continue to serve and bear witness in the common combat, to our anxiety to offer meaning and hope to all humanity. The metropolitan areas of the Ecumenical Patriarchate in all the countries of Europe, hundreds of parishes of Orthodox faithful in central and western Europe, made by emigrants but also of natives, belong to our flock, just as they are your people, entrusted to those who practice the art of politics. Moreover, beyond the actual limits of the European community of the Twelve, other nations with a very numerous population, in majority belonging to the Orthodox church tradition, follow in line with the European advance. Allow us to express the hope that these peoples also will be soon invited to participate in the life and institutions of united Europe.

The Ecumenical Patriarchate continues, through its faithful and from the nature of things, that there is a dimension essentially European in its ecumenical service. Beyond the ideological trends of each of you, despite the fact of personal metaphysical conviction or lack of convictions of each and everyone, we ask you to believe that the Ecumenical Patriarchate is entirely ready to offer its help to your effort for a united Europe, for a Europe which will not exist solely for itself but for the good of all humanity.

We wish to end with a prayer which in the Lenten season especially we Orthodox send up to the Prince of Peace: "Heavenly King, strengthen the faith; appease the nations; pacify the world."

This public discourse delivered by an eastern Orthodox Patriarch in a western European city, to an assembly to representatives of western governments, raises cogently and in a sophisticated manner the question of Europe and the Christian religion. Historians like Hilaire Belloc in *Europe and the Faith* and Christopher Dawson in *The Making of Europe* have shown how the Christian faith was influential in the origins. We seemed to return to this idealism with the birth of united Europe, after the Second World War. Those principally active in its promotion were committed Catholics, Alcide de Gasperi, Konrad Adenauer and Robert Schumann — which is not to overlook the contribution of Paul Spaak. Schumann was so exemplary that there is question of promoting his Beatification — he had experienced the tragedy of divided Europe in his personal life.

Pope Paul VI set a kind of seal on this concept by naming a special patron of Europe, very appropriately, St. Benedict. An interesting effect of the movement was the Franco-German Treaty signed by Adenauer and a Frenchman conspicuous for his nationalist spirit, Charles de Gaulle. The Treaty was signed in Rheims, a victim city of World War I, given a Christian character by attendance at Mass in the cathedral by the signatories. Pope John Paul II has maintained the religious aspect of the European movement by naming Saints Cyril and Methodius as joint patrons — this to emphasize the inclusion of the Eastern countries in the entity.

All this was in the domain of personal motivation with the original leaders. Was this ever convincingly shared with the masses? Has the initial impulse waned — so that economics, commercialism, and mere political rivalries have taken over? Was this a consequence of spreading secularism? Is there a way back or is it only under the impact of great catastrophes that people search for that which saves them? It is such questions that the deeply reflective views expressed by Bartholomew I to the European parliament may have prompted.

A practical step taken by him showed his willingness to translate words into action. On January 10, 1995, thanks to his initiative, the inauguration took place in Brussels of the Office of the Orthodox Church attached to the European Commission; it was a clean sign of the commitment of the Orthodox to united Europe — as Pius XII, in his time, had warmly supported the ideal. In May 1993, the Patriarch in Belgium had met Jacques Delors, then president of the Commission, who had requested the establishment of the Office. On the opening day, the president had sent a message which showed that the idealism of Robert Schumann had not died. Jacques Delors expressed his satisfaction that the Orthodox presence to the European institutions would be "more continuous and regular." "As you know," he continued "on my initiative, the European Commission has undertaken dialogue with the great Christian religions. ...After the construction of Europe centered on the economy, we are now in a new phase where the economic dimension alone will not suffice to sustain the European impetus."

The president had these words for the Orthodox: "At a time full of risks and difficulties, where not only freedom but cultural and national identities are threatened, Europe needs the contribution of the Orthodox Church, with its 200 million faithful, a majority in Greece and Eastern Europe, which constitutes a weighty power in the future of the continent."

Jacques Delors thought that Orthodoxy was called to serve as a bridge between East and West. It would be a "source of identity" for many Eastern Europeans, giving them the strength to resist the "temptations of exclusive nationalism;" it had condemned efforts to use religion for nationalist ends. The president thought that "Europeans of the West had much to receive from Orthodoxy, for it is an invitation to openness and to the dimension of transcendence which contributes to founding the very values on which the construction of Europe is based."

The Office is under the presidency of Metropolitan Panteleimon, representative of the Ecumenical Patriarchate in Belgium. Fr. Emmanuel Adamakis, appointed executive head of the Office, replied to the message which was delivered on behalf of the president of the European Commission. He expressed the wish that the Orthodox Church could participate in the construction of Europe; its system of values was the surest foundation for growth. It had faced the contemporary problems of social justice and the environment, particularly by "linking the theology of the person with the theology of society as a 'koinonia' (communion) of peoples."

Fr. Adamakis raised an important point. "The perspective of enlarging the European union towards the European countries of the East makes more relevant the responsibility of the Orthodox Church which is decisive in regard to the spiritual and cultural identity of these countries. It is the honor of the European Commission to have noted this very early dimension of the enlarged European union." He saw a future for the Office as it would allow the Orthodox to communicate the vision of man proper to their tradition, thus contributing to the search for a new model for European union.

In another way Bartholomew I was instrumental in creating a strong link between Orthodoxy and Europe. He helped to establish a center of Orthodox studies at university level in Munich where he had himself studied. Given full recognition and a highly qualified teaching staff this academic center will, with time, influence the intellectual world and enhance the position of the Orthodox in Europe. It is the first instance of a European state university setting up a complete course of Orthodox theological studies.

Light from the East

Chapter 7

Ecology

Bartholomew I, speaking to the European Parliament, was forthright in dealing with the ecological problem: "Allow me to express our conviction that the ecological problem of our century demands a radical revision of our cosmology...The Orthodox Church and theology are striving, in the measure of their spiritual powers, to offer a contribution to this problem by means of dialogue which, to their mind, is necessary. On the initiative of the Ecumenical Partriarchate, the Orthodox have established the 1st of September each year as a day of reflection and prayer with a view to facing the ecological catastrophe which threatens our planet."[1]

The initiative was taken by Dimitrios I in 1989; his objective was the protection of creation. His successor has resolutely followed his example.

In June, 1994, with Prince Philip, Duke of Edinburgh, president of the *World Wide Fund for Nature* (WWF), he sponsored a seminar on *Religious Training and Ecology*. It was held in the Orthodox monastery of the Holy Trinity on the island of Halki, off the Bosphorus, seat of the Institute of Theology of the Ecumenical Patriarchate, closed in 1971, awaiting reopening at the goodwill of the Turkish authorities. The seminar was attended by fifty representatives of different religious bodies and international associations.

The ten days were spent on exploring the relations between Orthodox spirituality and theology and the problems of the envi-

---

[1] SP., July-August, 1994.

ronment. Among the distinguished participants were William Reilly, former director of the USA agency for the protection of the environment and the Metropolitan of Pergamos, John Zizioulas, author of a book entitled *Creation as Eucharist: A Theological Approach to the Ecological Problem*. The essential objective was training: the aim was to influence parochial schools, preaching and theological teaching. Guidelines were drawn up.

In April, 1995, Bartholomew I combined his pastoral care for the Orthodox in the Far East with concern for the environment. He was invited by Prince Philip to participate in an international interconfessional symposium on problems of the environment and the protection of nature, which took place in the little Japanese island of Atami, facing Mount Fuji. The official title was *Religions and the Preservation of Nature*; a sequel was due to take place in Windsor Castle, some weeks later.

The voyage to Japan, the first by an Ecumenical Patriarch to the Far East, was the occasion of an encounter with the President of the Japanese Senate, an official reception, an encounter with Metropolitan Theodosios, primate of the autonomous Orthodox Church in Japan, and with ambassadors from the United States, Greece and Turkey.

From Japan, the Patriarch went on to South Korea. Here he visited different communities attached to the Ecumenical Patriarchate. He presided at the Sunday Eucharist in the Church of St. Nicholas in Seoul, and inaugurated important Orthodox centers. As everywhere he goes, he was received by the president of the country and the Minister for Culture, responsible for worship.

A symposium on the natural environment took place at the monastery of Halki, off the sea of Marmara, from July 1 through 7, 1996. It was under the joint patronage of the Ecumenical Patriarch, Bartholomew I and Prince Philip, Duke of Edinburgh, president of WWF (World Wildlife Fund). There were present theologians, scientists, specialists in the protection of nature from Europe, the United States, Canada, the Near East and Africa. Islam and Judaism were also represented. Two symposiums had been held in Halki in June 1994 and June 1995.

Messages expressing greetings and support were read from Prince Philip, Pope John Paul II, Archbishop George Carey of Canterbury, President Bill Clinton, and Jacques Santer, president of the European Commission. Prominent speakers were Metropolitan John of Pergamos, professor of theology at Thessalonica and King's College, London; Thomas Spencer, MEP, president of GLOBE International; and Laurence Mee, coordinator of the program for safeguarding the Black Sea.

The inaugural address was given by Patriarch Bartholomew I. He called for a mobilization of the moral and spiritual recourses of the entire human race to reestablish harmony between humankind and nature. He rejoiced at the growing interest given to problems of protecting the environment, especially among young people. He pleaded for a program to study in depth the "global threats" to nature due to "an irresponsible, even criminal" human mentality.

Bartholomew I announced the organization of an international symposium in the summer of 1997 on the subject of ecological needs of the Black Sea. The Ecumenical Patriarchate and WWF will in this have the cooperation of national foundations for the protection of nature in Greece and Turkey. The symposium will open in Athens and end in Istanbul, will take in meaningful visits to the countries bordering the Black Sea: Greece, Bulgaria, Romania, Moldavia, Ukraine, Russia, Georgia, Turkey.

Light from the East

Chapter 8

France

Early in his tenure of the patriarchate, Bartholomew I had occasion to travel to France. It was not an official visit to the state or the Catholic Hierarchy, such as he would make in 1995. His hosts were the Orthodox community. To them he spoke words which expressed his sense of Europe which we have seen, his institution of the French ethos and vision of a role for Orthodoxy in this setting. He felt "satisfaction and joy in hearing and seeing with his own eyes that there are Orthodox Christians living in the country that is France, who 'are standing firm in one spirit and one mind, as you are joined in conflict for the faith of the good news' (Philip 1:27)." His advice was couched in optimistic terms, but realistic:

"Preserve the unity of the Church and be witnesses to it, living in harmony with your canonical bishops, sharing in the same chalice, helping your love for all Christians, Orthodox and non-Orthodox, to grow. You, Orthodox in France, have the privilege of living in a country which in the past as in the present, guarantees tolerance, freedom of thought and action, a country which favors reflection and encourages creativity; a country, nonetheless which asks fundamental questions, decisive, existential questions. Confronted with the agonizing questions which men put to themselves today, Orthodox theology and spirituality must give their answer, their witness."

The Patriarch continued: "You are small in numbers. You have then the privilege and the mission to be the mustard seed...By your Baptism you have received the seal of the Cross, the seal of the

Lamb; you then have the mission, all without exception, to be the salt of this new Europe, to be its light."[1]

In November and December of the year 1995, Bartholomew I was active in the ecumenical world. From November 1 to 10, he was in France, guest of the Council of Christian Churches on the occasion of the centenary of the Greek Cathedral of Saint Etienne, rue Georges-Bizet, Paris. It was another "first" as no Ecumenical Patriarch had previously visited France. On the morning after his arrival, November 2, Bartholomew I was received at the Elysee by President Jacques Chirac. He informed journalists afterwards that in the hour and twenty minutes long meeting the two leaders had, in a warm atmosphere, spoken largely about three subjects: Turkey, which the Patriarch would like to see coming closer to the European Union; the project of reopening the Theological Institute at Halki, closed since 1971 by the government; and the situation of Orthodoxy throughout the world, especially in Eastern Europe.

The Patriarch went on to the Quai d'Orsay, where he exchanged views with the Minister for Foreign Affairs, Herve de Charette. In the evening he was in the Cathedral of Saint Etienne, to preside a doxology in the presence of ten bishops and many clergy and faithful. On November 3, there was a brief visit to the Armenian church in Paris and then an invitation from the Secretary General of UNESCO, Federico Mayor to take part in the twenty-eighth General Assembly of that body, and to address the members. In his discourse he had words of praise for the ideals of "tolerance, love and opposition to fragmentation" proper to the organization. Orthodoxy shares these ideals, he said and he regretted that in the eyes of some people Orthodoxy appeared "strange and remote." He denounced the egocentrism of societies and individuals. Man "was created to achieve self-fulfillment as a person in the 'image and likeness of God"; the true Self will only be found in the countenance of the other.

That evening the Patriarch was at the Reformed Church of Batignolles, to meet the heads of the French Protestant Federation. He paused for a moment's prayer in the Romanian Orthodox Chapel, which is housed by the Protestant parish. Then he was welcomed by Pastor Jacques Stewart, President of the Protestant Federation. Though

---

[1] DC., December 3, 1995, full texts.

protesting apologetically that he was more a canonist and a theologian, he spoke of St. John, "disciple of love, whose work shows that theology is not knowledge of the intellect, but a manifestation of the Holy Spirit." John taught "a mode of being, which does not depend on passing time. We await the glory of God, but we see it already. Does not the evangelist tell us that he has seen the kingdom?"

There are in western Europe parishes of Russian origin which have a special relationship with the Ecumenical Patriarchate. Their archbishop, presently Serge, has his cathedral, Saint Alexandre de la Neva in Rue Daru, Paris. There on Saturday, November 4, the Patriarch celebrated the Eucharistic liturgy, with the Archbishop Serge and his two Auxiliary bishops Paul and Michel, with Macaire, Auxiliary of the Swiss Diocese of the Ecumenical Patriarchate and Stephane, Auxiliary of the French Diocese of the Patriarchate. About thirty priests and very many lay delegates from all the parishes of the archdiocese were in the church and were presented to the Patriarch by Archbishop Serge. The Patriarch expressed his joy and emotion at seeing that different generations of Russian emigration "had been able to make the presence of Orthodoxy living and impressive among the Christians of the West."

In the afternoon, Bartholomew I went to the St. Serge Institute, where he was awarded a Doctorate *honoris causa*. He emphasized the contribution made by the great Institute to Orthodox thought and witness, especially in its commitment to ecumenical dialogue. "Today," in his address to the professors and students, he said, "Orthodoxy is having temptations of fear, of distrust, of isolation. This is but a fit of passing fever. You are the witnesses to an Orthodoxy which is living, open, creative 'for the life of the world.'" The day ended with a concert of liturgical music in the Church of Saint-Sulpice; three choirs honored the Patriarch: the Byzantine Choir of Greece, conducted by Lycourgos Angelopoulos; the Paris St. Serge Choir, conducted by Nicolas Ossorguine and that of the Antiochian Vicariate conducted by Elie Khoury.

On Sunday, November 5, Bartholomew I presided over the Eucharistic liturgy in the Greek Cathedral of Saint Etienne, which marked the commemoration of the centenary. With the Patriarch were his Metropolitan in France Jeremie and the latter's Auxiliary, Stephanos as well as these Metropolitans: Damaskinos from Switzerland, Constantin from Derka, Cyrillos from Seleucia, and Michael from Austria; with them were Archbishop Serge and Bishop Damaskin of the French Serbian Church. Eight other bishops represented the dioceses of the Ecumenical Patriarchate in western Europe; and there were several priests from different communions and several hundred faithful.

Bartholomew I chose St. Stephen Martyr as the theme of his homily. "Unity," he maintained, did not come from "the law of the strongest," but from "humility and pardon," which are "the highest form of communion." "Accomplish works of love, love one another, avoid quarrel and rivalries, seek faith in humility, love in faith, and hope in love which does not fade."

In the afternoon, the visitor from the East was received in the splendid Catholic Cathedral of Paris, Notre Dame. Cardinal Lustiger first met him and together they entered this hallowed place of worship, through which so much history has, down the ages, flowed. Orthodox Vespers were celebrated in Greek, Slav and French before a congregation of Orthodox, Catholics and Protestants estimated at 5,000. The presence of faithful from the different Churches prompted the Patriarch to speak of the Will of God manifest. He pleaded for mutual knowledge and understanding, which would be possible only through love which pardons in the example of Christ, "from the Cross He pardons His executioners and in them all sinful humanity, bearing our sins, He is the only one without sin who suffered for all."

Patriarch and Cardinal prayed for peace in the Middle East and they spoke of their emotion at the news of the assassination of the Israeli Prime Minister, Yitzhak Rabin, which had occurred the day before.

From Paris to Lourdes where leaders of Catholic France awaited the Patriarch, where he would have an encounter second only in importance to his meeting with the Pope earlier in the year. He had made history by addressing the European Parliament, as we have seen. Now he would also do so by meeting and addressing the collective episcopate of one of the oldest Catholic countries in the world, the oldest in Europe as the commemoration of Clovis reminds us this year.

On November 6, in presence of the full assembly the president, Mgr. Joseph Duval welcomed the Patriarch in a lengthy address in which the most serious problems and the most encouraging movements were frankly and lucidly set forth. Some extracts may be quoted:

> We welcome you in this Marian city of Lourdes, known throughout the whole world as one of those places where the Mother of God, the *Theotokos,* came to remind us of the Gospel summons to conversion and prayer, and to show herself as one all pure and all Immaculate...Could we fail to think especially of her meeting with Elizabeth related to St. Luke? Is this not for us the archetype of a true meeting of Christians? Every encounter between those who answer the calls of God opens sooner or later on the joy of a *Magnificat*? Is it not also the model of the missionary service of everyone baptized by Christ, bearing Christ to reveal Him to the world?...in the womb of the Church of which Mary is the perfect figure we know and love the one in whom we believe without having seen him. In this light of the mystery of the Visitation we grasp the spiritual dimension of your traveling through the whole world to meet not only your Orthodox brothers and sisters, but also other Christians and every person of goodwill. We gratefully remember your recent 'visitation' to His Holiness Pope John Paul II, himself too a tireless pilgrim for unity and peace.
>
> We receive you as a brother in the Lord, we salute you as bishop of the first See of Orthodoxy, and through you we salute the entire Orthodox Church, which without hesitation we call a Sister Church.
>
> The Orthodox Church and the Catholic Church are rooted in the apostolic preaching, in the heritage of the Church undivided. For our part we declare that when you celebrate the Eucharist, you celebrate it in its fullness and by it the whole Church is built up.
>
> We believe that in the Orthodox Church and in the Catholic Church, deacons, priests and bishops receive the same ministry, each according to the hierarchical order, and celebrate the same sacraments.

No Catholic, since the teachings of the Second Vatican Council can any longer doubt these realities.

The first results of the work of the Joint International Commission for Catholic Orthodox dialogue give us hope that the day is not far away when our two Churches will together officially proclaim such statements.

Our theologians' research remains necessary even if it is but a poor human contribution to our welcome for the divine gift of full communion...

"We have already made much progress in the necessary mutual knowledge among the faithful, but we cannot conceal our sadness to note still often in certain Orthodox countries a surprising failure to recognize the true spiritual riches of our Catholic Church, which does not seek for all that to deny its own weaknesses, nor her share of responsibility in the dramatic separations between East and West.

Your Holiness, by your long ecumenical experience and great openness of mind and heart you encourage us to continue on the path of mutual discovery and enrichment, despite the ignorance which remains here and there.

For us Catholics this testimony (already mentioned in regard to the unity and universality of Orthodoxy) is most precious, for it allows us to help our faithful to understand better our Orthodox brothers and sisters.

To live in a harmony between unity and diversity is a crucial difficulty for each of our Churches. Orthodoxy has pushed diversity to its extreme, but the very existence of the Ecumenical Patriarchate, the initiatives of Your Holiness, and those of the other Orthodox Patriarchs, as also the preparation for the Pan-Orthodox Council, bring a certain sense of balance.

Catholicism, for its part, has pushed unity to its extreme, but the Synods of bishops and episcopal conferences are bringing progressively the needed complement, or even correction.

Mgr. Duval elaborated this idea suggesting that Catholics and Orthodox need each other. He did not shirk the painful point: "Is not here the true serious problem still remaining between us; that of the inter-relationship between the local and regional primacies and the universal primacy, all to serve together the unique communion?

"In France, Catholics and Orthodox pursue their cooperation and their dialogue in serenity, confidence and friendship. The joint commission of Catholic-Orthodox dialogue does useful work. I am thinking especially of its study of the Roman primacy in the reflection of the Churches and the actual reflection on uniatism."

Mgr. Duval gave evidence of Orthodox participation in all the ecumenical movements, as he briefly recalled the Orthodox immigration from different countries to France since the nineteenth century. France has benefited culturally therefrom. He quoted names of Orthodox writers who influenced either French writers (Nicholas Berdyaev on Maritain, Mounier, Danielou) or French religious life, Soljenitsyn especially. The Orthodox have helped French Catholics to discover the Fathers of the Church and Icons. Recalling Bartholomew I's pledge to pursue dialogue given on the day of his enthronement and the kindred conviction of John Paul II, Mgr. Duval looked forward to the day when Christians united would in the strength of unity bring Christ to the millions suffering from the evils of our time.

The Patriarch's reply was on the same spiritual level, which meant that it was entirely idealistic and relevant to life. He spoke of the situation of the Patriarchate, few faithful, "no temporal power or protection." But he recalled the words of the Apostle, "My strength comes to perfection where there is weakness" (2 Cor. 12:9). And he appealed to the mighty witness of history surrounding Constantinople — the General Councils held within its jurisdiction in the first millennium, its evangelizing influence spreading far and wide.

Bartholomew I showed thorough awareness of the essential moments in French history. It was the very excellence of French Catholicism that exposed it to the challenge of the "phenomenon of atheism" in the upheaval of the Revolution, in which the triumph was all the more remarkable. He related the achievement of French theology recognized by all with knowledge of these things to valued awareness of Orthodox theology, evident in scholarly centers. He mentioned also, as a precious accompaniment, the expertise of French Catholic scientists, naming Louis Pasteur, Alexis

Carrel, Maurice de Broglie and Pierre-Paul Grasse. He had a special mention of Pierre Teilhard Chardin, as he had for those who articulated Catholic thought in the political area, Robert Schumann and Jacques Delors. He paid a warm tribute to Mgr. Pierre Duprey, active in the Pontifical Council for Christian Unity. All together the episcopate of France was exemplary in its ecumenical concern, especially in regard to the Orthodox. All this was in line with his original assertion that the Orthodox was not a *static* Church.

The Patriarch made another memorable address, when he spoke in the Basilica of Our Lady of the Rosary during the religious office celebrated by the French bishops. Here he spoke as heir to the mighty Marian tradition of the East, of the *Theotokos*. He spoke of Mary's intercession, of her mediation after the mediation of Christ, and he ended with quotations from the St. Gregory Palamas, made known to the contemporary world by Fr. John Meyerndorff, recently deceased, the ornament of St. Vladimir's seminary, New York. One example: "The Mother of God, is, after Christ, while still being with him and because of her unity with him, the thought of the prophets, the head of Apostles and the certainty of doctors. She is the glory of whatever is human, the enchantment of things celestial, the ornament of all creation. She is the principle, the source and the root of ineffable good things, the summit and fulfillment of all that is holy."

This last phrase presenting the Virgin as the summit and fulfillment of all that is holy bears witness to the importance of her person and her wonderful achievement. "She has surpassed all human nature, she remains the summit of holiness, being the goal of all holiness, for, according to the Fathers, God bestows His gifts through the mediation of Mary." Here the Patriarch is more explicit on Mary's mediation to God than he had been earlier in his homily — we have seen that this thesis is very strong among the Palamites. "The love and respect which we manifest towards the Mother of God are indissolubly linked with the love and respect we harbor for her Son and God." How wonderfully these words of the Patriarch echo the mighty traditions of the East.

Refreshed spiritually no doubt by the Virgin of Lourdes and comforted by the solidarity shown him by the French bishops, the Patriarch was able to fulfill a very heavy program in visits to the cities of Marseille, Aix, Nice and Monaco. He was greeted by the

Orthodox faithful in these cities, notably in Marseille, was given all the honors, civil and ecclesiastical. He was received by the Senayor Mayor of Marseille and found time to offer some reflections on the links between the city and Greece, enlarging his thought to deal with the problems of great cities. As everywhere he has been, he avoided clichés and routine formalities, leaving behind him words to remember and ponder.

Welcomed in the Basilica of St. Victor by the Archbishop of Marseille, Mgr. Bernard Panafieu, and the Archbishop of Aix and Arles, Mgr. Louis-Marie Bille, the Patriarch invited Christians to wake up and, leaving sterile discussions, engage in a dialogue of love. Mgr. Panafieu and the "Cure" of the Basilica presented to him a relic of St. John Cassian, a fourth century monk whose life was lived in Egypt, Palestine, Constantinople and Rome. Next day it was a service in the Church of St. Irenaeus to commemorate a devoted Orthodox priest, founder of the parish, a zealous servant of Orthodoxy in France (d.1994). Then Bartholomew I went to the Faculty of Law and Economics of the University of Aix-Marseille to receive an honorary doctorate in Canon Law.

Arriving by plane in Nice in the afternoon, he went to the Greek Church of Saint Spyridon, where he was welcomed by Bishop Stephanos. Presiding at a doxology in the open air he spoke of "peace, love and tolerance." Referring to European progress in economics and technology he asserted that "it was necessary to brighten the light of human reason with the joyous light of the Lord." Then he took part in an ecumenical prayer in Nice Senior Seminary along with Mgr. Francois Saint-Macary, Bishop of Nice. He met the city mayor, Jacques Peyrat. Later, he presided over a doxology in the Russian Cathedral of Saint Nicholas; he encouraged the Orthodox community to remain faithful to their cultural and religious roots.

The next day, the tireless visitor was in Monaco. First he presided over a solemn ecumenical celebration in the Church of St. Nicholas of Fontvieille. With him were Mgr. Joseph Sardo, Archbishop of Monaco, Mgr. Macary, Bishop of Nice, Pastor Louis Schloesing, president of the regional council of the Reformed Church of France, Fr. Kenneth Letts of the Anglican Parish of Nice, Mgr. Daron, Armenian Bishop of Marseille and Dom Nicholas, Abbot of Lerins. Bartholomew I stated, "We must agree according to Christ, in Christ and through Christ" to do which "boldness and courage are needed"; "the Lord holds out a helping hand and is waiting for centuries that we grasp it." There was also a celebration in the cathedral, attended by Prince Albert. Before leaving Monaco, Bartholomew I was received in the official residence by Prince Rainier and the government of the Principality.

Back in Paris on November 9, the Patriarch met representatives of the Georgian Orthodox and the Ukrainian Orthodox in France. Then he met a delegation from the Universal Israeli Alliance headed by their President Professor Steg and the Chief Rabbi, Joseph Strug. He wished to promote "understanding between the Orthodox Churches and Judaism." He spoke to some hundreds of young Orthodox faithful; he was honored by Rene Monory, President of the Senate, in the Luxembourg Palace and by Jean Tiberi, Mayor of Paris in the Hotel de Ville.

Thus was concluded an important series of events. The response to the first visit from an Ecumenical Patriarch to Church and State in France had been most impressive. He had spoken some fifty times and never on any level but that of the highest spirituality, with a compelling theological clarity and a challenge to the profound instinct of the faith. We are here a long way from the power struggle which precipitated the break in 1054. At that time, one met no appeal to the words of the Master, no readiness to follow his teaching as Bartholomew I so evidently manifests.

We have seen that already on two occasions the Patriarch was prepared to give a press conference, to face the media — the first in his position to do so in a western country. He did so again on November 9 before leaving France. His fundamental principle was stated at the outset: "The most powerful sentiment, the only one which justifies a man being qualified as human is love of everyone; hatred is a destructive force; it serves neither the one who hates nor the one who is hated; solutions will be found through dialogue and never by violence" he explained, adding that this principle enunciated for ex-Yugoslavia, applied also to inter-Orthodox relations and to the search for unity among Christians.

Bartholomew I, conscious of his office thought it well to issue a clear statement of outlook and policy in the face of so much media discussion of the war in ex-Yugoslavia; inevitably some journalists seized on the religious factor.

Chapter 9

Estonia

It may seem strange to introduce a controversial matter which arose between the Patriarchate of Constantinople and that of Moscow concerning the Baltic state of Estonia with a quotation from Pope John Paul II. It helps to set the stage. The Pope, on September 15, 1994, received in official audience Mr. Lennert Mere, President of the country. "After the painful period of suffering marked especially by the denial of basic human freedom, the Estonia nation" the Pope said, "is now living in a climate of moral and civil rebirth." The Pope himself had lived through a similar "period of suffering" in his own country. Later in his address he spoke thus: "Mr. President, thanks to the harmony that exists between them, the various Christian confessions present in your country also help to encourage a climate of peace and cooperation. The ecumenical meeting held in the Church of St. Nicholas, in which I had the joy to take part during my previously mentioned Pastoral Visit, was an eloquent sign of the commitment of all those who profess a common faith in Christ to continue seriously on their journey towards full unity. Their witness to Gospel values helps keep alive the memory of the great cultural and human patrimony that Christianity historically offered to the civilization and progress of the Baltic people, especially to Estonians." The Pope spoke of "the still gaping wounds in people's minds. They are the sad legacy of the long winter of totalitarian oppression." The Pope referred to the geographical location of Estonia which makes it a place of "cultural and religious dialogue" between the different peoples of Europe. "In this regard," he added, "my sincere wish is that the tension and conflicts may be completely overcome once for all, leaving room for a generous exchange between the many cultures for the sake of their mutual enrichment. May the rediscovery of common Christian roots, the inviolable heritage of every nation of the old continent, become the starting-point for renewed dialogue and closer cooperation between Eastern and Western Europe."

Within a short time it could have appeared that one source of tension would disappoint the Pope's wish and endanger the mutual enrichment which he foresaw. Estonia is largely Lutheran, but there is an Orthodox Church whose membership is about one quarter that of the Protestant body. These faithful have suffered vicissitudes with the changing political situation in their country. In 1918 the Orthodox Bishop Platon of Tallinn, capital and largest city of the country urged the Orthodox to support the underground Estonian independence movement, not the German occupying forces or the Russian Bolsheviks. He was assassinated by Estonian Bolsheviks and is rightly honored as a martyr. After his death, his Church in Estonia came under the jurisdiction of the Ecumenical Patriarch in Constantinople.

Things changed with the Soviet occupation of Estonia in 1940. The Orthodox Church in the country was brought under the Moscow Patriarchate; active dissidents succeeded in setting up an "Estonian Church in Exile," based in Stockholm. Stalin, in the pressing needs of World War II, restored the Orthodox Church, with limitations; the only Orthodox Church allowed was the Russian. All the real estate owned by the Estonian Apostolic Orthodox Church was confiscated; parishes of the Russian Orthodox Church in Estonia had to pay rent to the state for the use of church buildings. The Russian Orthodox Church in the country survived nonetheless. So closely was it kept linked with Moscow that an Estonian became the Patriarch of the whole Church, Aleksei II.

The link with Moscow was not to survive the collapse of the Marxist regime. The independent government did not want a quarrel with Russia, but had no enthusiasm for dependence on it in any department of Estonian life. Activists in favor of a return to the Ecumenical Patriarchate worked at home and made their case at the World Council of Churches meeting at Canberra in 1991. The Ecumenical Patriarch decided that he should take back the Orthodox in Estonia under his ecclesial protection. As people could read in the world's press and hear and see on the media this action provoked a crisis, a break between Constantinople and Moscow. Fortunately, it was not of long duration. The point of eruption was in February, 1996; a modus vivendi was agreed on in May of that year. Much negotiation took place with the happy outcome that the Orthodox in Estonia could choose their allegiance, either to Moscow, with which some were ethically identified, or with Constantinople. The sympathizers with Russia had a determined leader Archbishop Kornilli (Cornelius) of Tallinn. The reader may be interested in the official press releases from Moscow and Istanbul.

The crisis date is thus stated in the press release of the Moscow Patriarchate: Today, on February 23, 1996, the name day of the Patriarch of Moscow, during the divine liturgy celebrated in the Moscow Patriarchal Cathedral of the Epiphany, His Holiness Patriarch Alexy II of Moscow and all Russia did not pronounce the name of the Patriarch Bartholomaios, Primate of the Orthodox Church of Constantinople among the names of the Primates of the local Orthodox Churches. It has been done for the first time in 1008 years' history of the Russian Orthodox Church.

This action witnessed the breaking of Orthodox unity which has been existing for centuries and became a tragedy for Orthodox believers. It is the culmination of the conflict which has been growing around the situation of the Orthodox Church in Estonia during the last years. Part of the Russian Orthodox Church was under the pressure of the Estonian government aiming to make Russian speaking Orthodox believers leave the country. The Orthodox Church in Estonia was denied official registration; at the same time clergy and parishioners were not allowed to have contacts with the Mother Russian Church. All this is extreme violation of basic human rights, religious liberty, the main principles of democratic society.

The most tragic part of it is the fact that in the most difficult situation the acts of the Estonian government aimed at the weakening and splitting of Orthodoxy were supported by the Patriarchate of Constantinople, which is wishing to spread its power to the believers in that country. Yesterday, February 22, 1996, the Holy Synod of the Russian Orthodox Church discussing the situation, expressed its strong disapproval of the intentions of Constantinople to take under its jurisdiction the schismatic group of clergy and lay people who are supported by the Estonian government. The urgent telegram to Patriarch Bartholomaios said. 'This act would not only divide the Orthodox Church in Estonia, but at the same time it would deepen the suffering of those Orthodox whose rights have been violated. We are brotherly warning your Holiness that in case of the fulfillment of your intentions, your Holiness is taking upon yourself the heavy responsibility for the tragic division of Orthodoxy at the time of the approaching 200th anniversary of Christianity.

Yesterday, February 22, 1996, without listening to the appeal made by the Russian Orthodox Church, with the approval of the ruling power, the foundation of a new Estonian Church was announced under the jurisdiction of Constantinople. Such actions are the most cruel violations of all main canonical rules existing in the Orthodox world, as well as the invasion of the territory of another local Orthodox Church.

The press release from the Ecumenical Patriarchate on the course of action followed:

On February 20, 1996, the Holy and Sacred Synod of the Ecumenical Patriarchate was convened and presided over by his All Holiness Ecumenical Partriarch Bartholomew. Deliberating in the Holy Spirit, the Synod unanimously decided, by Patriarchal and Synodical Act, to declare the reactivation of the Tome of 1923 which had been issued during the tenure of Ecumenical Patriarch Meletios IV. This Tome had established, under the Ecumenical Patriarchate the Autonomous Orthodox Apostolic Church of Estonia known as "Orthodox Metropolitanate of Estonia." Due to the then existing political conditions and following the persistent request of the Patriarch of Moscow, the Tome was declared inoperative in 1978.

The Ecumenical Patriarchate has assigned the neighboring Archbishop John of Karelia and all Finland as Locum Tenens of the reinstated Orthodox Metropolitanate of Estonia. Archbishop John will oversee the restructuring of the Metropolitanate *ad referendum* to the Ecumenical Patriarchate, which will then proceed with the election and installation of the canonical hierarchs of the Metropolitanate.

The Ecumenical Patriarchate proceeded with this decision following the persistent request of the Estonian government and the overwhelming majority of the Estonian Orthodox parishes, which requested they be placed again under the aegis of the Ecumenical Patriarchate. The said parishes declared categorically that even if the Ecumenical Patriarchate declined to receive them, under no condition would they remain any longer under the Patriarchate of Moscow.

It is noted that in 1945 the Autonomous Church of Estonia was unilaterally and forcibly abolished by the Patriarchate of Moscow, following the annexation, under the might of weapons, of Estonia to the Soviet Union. At that time, the Primate of the Autonomous Orthodox Church of Estonia was compelled along with the clergy and laity of his Church to establish itself in Sweden as head of the Autonomous Orthodox Church of Estonia in Exile. Having regained political independence as a country, the reinstitution of the Autonomous Orthodox Church of Estonia, forcibly abolished as indicated above, constituted a just request of the Estonian Orthodox. To this just request the Mother Church, the Ecumenical Patriarchate, out of a sense of responsibility and by canonical right, was duty-bound to respond with compassion and in their defense.

This request of the Estonian government and the Estonian Orthodox clergy and laity met with opposition by His Beatitude the Patriarch Alexy of Moscow and all Russia, even though, as has firmly been the case in Orthodoxy, all autocephalous and autonomous Orthodox Churches were so declared, always according to the demand of the governments of the countries of these Churches, as well as of their clergy and laity.

In its effort to avoid all antagonism within the bosom of the Orthodox Church, the Ecumenical Patriarchate entered into bilateral discussions with the Most Holy Church of Russia that they might reach a solution of compromise acceptable to all. Unfortunately, due to the intransigent position of the Patriarchate of Moscow, these discussions, pursued over a two-year period, did not bring about any positive results.

Following this, the Ecumenical Patriarchate recognized that it cannot be permitted to:

a) either betray the centuries-old tradition regarding the means and conditions by which autonomous and autocephalous Churches are instituted;

b) or overlook the right of the Estonian Orthodox Church which by a two-thirds majority — more than 67% — over which the Church of Russia has exercised unbearable pressure through continual punishment and sanctions, adamantly demands to reinstitute the operation of the former status of ecclesiastical autonomy in effect prior to 1945 when it was abolished by the Soviets; or overlook the similar, unyielding demand of the Government of Estonia;

c) or, finally, to obliterate the future of Orthodoxy in the modern world, a world which seeks Orthodoxy, through actions which would project it as essentially either Slavonic or Greek, so that those wishing to embrace Orthodoxy need first to be Greek or Russian; this would prove most disastrous for Orthodoxy and its message.

With a painful soul the Ecumenical Patriarchate chose not to side with the mighty of the earth, but to uphold justice and responsibility. The Patriarchate prays for one and only one thing, that by all means the name of our Lord Jesus Christ be magnified and that Orthodoxy by glorified.

Pursuing love and peace with all, excluding no one and in particular the Patriarchate of Moscow and its Primate His Beatitude Patriarch Alexy, the Church of Constantinople declared with joy and delight that it will accept whatever positive proposals the Church of Russia might offer for the good of the Estonian Orthodox Autonomous Church, and for a better settlement of all matters concerning her.

(At the Patriarchate, February 24, 1996, from the Chief Secretariat of the Holy and Sacred Synod.)

Light from the East

Chapter 10

Ethiopia

Patriarch Abuna Paul, Primate of the Prechalcedonian Orthodox Church in Ethiopia visited, in December, 1993, Bartholomew
I in the Phanar. In answer to an invitation from him, the Ecumenical Patriarch went on a visit to Ethiopia from January 11 to 21,
1995, the first in history from Constantinople to Addis Abeba. The
encounter has to be seen in the general context of the current rapprochement between the Orthodox Church within the jurisdiction
of Constantinople and the Prechalcedonian Churches. A joint theological commission is at work on this task of reconciliation; it had
published two declarations, in 1989 and 1990. The Ecumenical
Patriarch was also actuated by a motive of brotherly solidarity with
the Church in Ethiopia, which had much to suffer during the regime of Mengistu, still suffers from divisions caused by interference from other Churches.

The visiting Patriarch was greeted enthusiastically by very
large crowds in Addis Abeba and Axoum. He went to some of the
most ancient churches and monasteries in the country. He was
received by the President, Meles Zenawi and the Prime Minister,
Tamrat Layne.

An important moment was the working session between the
Patriarch's delegation and the members of the Ethiopian Holy
Synod. Questions of actuality over a wide range were discussed.
Bartholomew I thought that "theological dialogue between Ortho-
dox and prechalcedonians was moving forward satisfactorily to-

wards the re-establishment of full communion." A declaration signed at the end of the visit by the Ecumenical Patriarch and Abuna Paul showed the identity of opinions of the two Churches. It was agreed that the decisions of the Joint Theological Commission for Dialogue between the Orthodox Church and Eastern Orthodox Churches should be accepted and given validity.

Chapter 11

Georgia

From May 6 to 9, Bartholomew I paid an official visit to the Patriarchate of Georgia. He was received by Elias II, Patriarch-Catholicos, Primate of the Orthodox Church of Georgia as well as many other personalities. He was overjoyed to see the Orthodoxy had risen again in the area, impressed too that his visit took on the character of a national event. The president, Edward Chevardnadze spoke of it as *historic*.

Speaking to the Patriarch Elias II, Bartholomew I rejoiced that "for the first time in two centuries, not only is Georgia an independent state, but the autocephalous and patriarchal rank of the Church are recognized by all and atheism belongs to the sad memories of the past." The Orthodox Church had great responsibility, he said, and he appealed for absolute respect for one's neighbor, seeing that freedom's limits are marked where another's freedom begins — a golden rule, valid for persons and for peoples.

President Chevardnadze was warmhearted in his meeting with Bartholomew I. He emphasized the attachment of the Georgian nation to Orthodox tradition; he hoped that Orthodoxy would provide the solution to the problems the country was currently facing, not, he added "a crisis of thinking, but a collapse of ideologies." Then he made a touching personal remark, "Stalin began in a seminary only to become a communist, declaring that God does not exist. I was a communist and was to become a Christian."

The reply of Bartholomew matched this frankness, adding a dimension of spirituality: "The world awaits a new, dynamic outline of civilization, one which will transform church experience and the hope of vital intervention. If an economy controlled by centralized power has produced the horror of totalitarianism, the so-called liberal economy patently produces societies which are anti-social with monstrous egocentrism, violence and the pitiless law of the strongest." He added, "Unfortunately, we Orthodox have not worked sufficiently to formulate, for example, what scheme of political economy flows from our tradition and our vision of humanity."

In a meeting with young people, the Patriarch denounced "the confusion, uncertainty and clashes which today tyrannize the countries of eastern Europe" but regretted that these problems are largely due to the fact that "the Orthodox have not been able to bring a realistic solution to the question as to what it means to be Orthodox today in a world subject without restraint to technology, to an absolute regard for economic priorities, a world where the individual is divinised, where there is idolatry of productivity, where the hysteria of consumerism reigns."

On May 8, the Eucharist was celebrated by the two Patriarchs, before a fervent assembly, Bartholomew I's theme was Orthodox unity. "History leaves deep wounds and often feeds distrust among peoples. But this distrust should have no place in the Church; it could easily poison relations between Orthodox, and deprive Orthodoxy of the cohesion which is today absolutely necessary to it, as the need is more and more understood for Panorthodox unity which will assume responsibility for harmonious cooperation with a view towards the unity of the autocephalous local churches." The Patriarch insisted that he was not speaking from a power center, but one of unity, faithful in this to Orthodox theology of the Church.

His visit was an event for the Orthodox in Georgia, the second by an Ecumenical Patriarch — the first dated from 1987. The Church in this region goes back to the fourth century and has had much to endure through the ages. It lost its autocephalous dignity in 1811, after the seizure by Russia in 1801. There was a period of intense persecution during the Soviet regime. In 1943, the Patriarch of Moscow fully recognized its autocephalous status and in 1990 the Ecumenical Patriarch did likewise. There are fifteen dioceses, an academy of theology, opened in 1989 and a seminary in Tiflis. The faithful may number two and a quarter million.

Chapter 12

Commemoration of the Apocalypse

One must never forget in thinking of the Orthodox that they have a consciousness of the first age of our Church not given to us in the West. They live in the countries where Christianity was born and first grew, where the first great theological debates were active and engaged the teaching authority of the Church in General Councils. With this in mind, we can look at the celebrations of the Apocalypse of St. John which took place in 1995, nineteenth centenary of the composition of the Apocalypse, the book of Revelation which is the last separate work in the New Testament. All that is here recorded was due to the initiative of Bartholomew I.[1]

The commemoration was held on the island of Patmos, where tradition says that St. John resided during the persecution of Domitian (81-96 A.D.). Patriarchs or Archbishops of the Churches within reasonable distance of the island were personally present or represented. Only the Patriarch of Moscow and the Metropolitan of Warsaw did not respond to Bartholomew I's invitation. All first met on September 23, in the Monastery of St. John the Evangelist for a short doxology, over which the Patriarch presided. He spoke of the "inexhaustible treasury of tradition which rests permanently on the word and sacraments of the Church." He warned against false interpretations of the book of the Apocalypse; the revelation

---

1   SP., November, 1995.

given for the salvation of all humankind can be explained and taught only in the light of liturgical and sacramental experience and in drawing on the theological legacy of the Fathers of the Church.

It was the Serb Patriarch Paul I who presided over the Sunday Eucharistic celebration in the Church of the Mother of God in the village of Chora, overlooked by the Monastery of St. John. He pleaded for prayers for all the victims of war in ex-Yugoslavia, "It is the duty of Christians to pardon everyone and to show compassion for the pains of those who suffer."

After the liturgy, the whole morning was spent in a summit of the Orthodox Primates which continued on the morning of September 25. A declaration was issued; it will merit attention presently. Meanwhile, in the afternoon of September 24 another important project initiated by Bartholomew I, with the support of Prince Philips reached its conclusion. An international scientific symposium on "Revelation (the Apocalypse) and the Environment from 95 to 1995," had begun from Athens on September 20 on a cruise through the Aegean. The purpose was to study the ecological relevance of the Apocalypse and to induce Christian leaders to have greater concern for the environment and the protection of nature. The Patriarch had been with the symposium members on board the *Moni Prevellis* until he left at the port of Kusadasi to reach Patmos. From the 17th to the 22nd of the month, a symposium, likewise under the aegis of the Patriarch, with the cooperation of Athens University, had taken place in Athens on the influence of the Apocalypse on the sciences and arts.

The symposium on the environment was attended by a hundred members, with Metropolitan John of Pergamos as coordinator, and as lecturers Bishop Kallistos of Diokleia, Bishop Nifon of Slobozia (Romania), Metropolitan Athenagoras of Fokis (Greece), Christos Yannaras, Greek Orthodox layman, a philosopher and professor at the Athens Institute of Political Sciences, and John Foundolis, professor at the faculty of Theology in Thessalonica. Cardinal Roger Etchegaray, President of the Pontifical Council for Justice and Peace represented the Catholic Church, Dr. Richard Chartres, Bishop of Stepney the Anglican Church. Present also were Timothy Wirth, American Under-Secretary of State, executive director for UNO environment program and Elizabeth Dowdeswell, president of the

Turkish association for the protection of marine resources. The symposium was placed under a varied high patronage.

Metropolitan John of Pergamos, summarizing the results of the symposium evoked texts from the Apocalypse with a bearing on their subject. He concluded his reflections thus: "The solution of ecological problems is not a simple technical problem of management, but it calls for a total change in our vision of the world and our ideologies."

Winding up the symposium in Patmos, the Patriarch stated his main conviction thus: "Destructive deterioration threatens the environment in many ways. We can no longer be satisfied with verbal protests; each one must find ways of acting more and more concretely against a pollution which will tomorrow be impossible to control if we remain inactive." He announced the setting up, in the near future, in Patmos of an international ecological center, operating under the aegis of the Ecumenical Patriarchate; it will favor close cooperation between specialists in ecology, Church authorities and theologians.

The participants in the symposium would like to see a new sin defined "against nature." They thought that governments and scientists were not sufficiently attentive to protection of the marine milieu; they deplored the French nuclear tests, which would impel other nuclear powers to continue developing their arms, ending in a proliferation of weapons and nuclear war.

The Athenian symposium on the influence of the Apocalypse on the sciences and arts was attended by forty highly qualified people, from universities, theologians, specialists in literature and the history of art: half from Greece and half from European countries. They dealt with contemporary exegesis of the Apocalypse, its impact on history and on the pictorial arts in Europe and America. The participants reached Patmos by boat.

Here the climax to the commemoration was an open air Eucharistic Liturgy in which the Ecumenical Patriarch was joined by the other Primates as concelebrants. It was celebrated near the grotto of the Apocalypse where, according to tradition, St. John received the revelation. Three thousand faithful were present and a thousand visitors or guests. At the end of the liturgy, the Primates were in solemn procession to the grotto. Bartholomew I, in his solemn address spoke of the reality of history in John's Revelation, "all its tragedies, threats, pollutions, disasters, injustices — but also with all its mercy, grace and rest" which come from God. "If we, men and women of the modern world," he said, "often experience the calamities of which Saint John speaks in his Apocalypse we are nevertheless deprived of the source of salvation, for every genuine revelation within the Church is a personal experience in the Spirit, ... a gift of God to His creation."

The program included visits to the Orthodox school of Theology in Patmos and to the feminine monastic community in the Monastery of the Annunciation, an illuminated and sound-track record of the history of Patmos and a concert of liturgical song in the Byzantine, Slav and Georgian tradition. The government was fully supportive. The Greek president, Costis Stephanopoulos offered a banquet in honor of the Primates, and the Prime Minister. Andreas Papandreou, with many members of the government were present.

An important document emanated from the event. Participants in the summit published a declaration which they deemed it their duty to issue in "these times of crisis which many characterize as apocalyptic." It was, they thought, their duty to "emphasize what Revelation in Christ means for the progress of humanity." It is their responsibility to contribute "morally and spiritually to peace, justice and the brotherhood of peoples." The authors of the text were at pains to repudiate an "erroneous or distorted image" of Orthodoxy. "Let it be quite clear to all that the Orthodox perception of the idea of nation does not in any way contain the slightest element of aggressiveness or confrontation between peoples...nationalism is a phenomenon totally foreign to the Orthodox Church...we condemn all fanatical nationalism, which could lead to division and hatred between peoples"; the Primates denounced all attacks against "the cultural rights, freedom or the dignity of all minorities."

In this important document among the important events affecting Orthodoxy in the present century, there is first a tribute to the Orthodox victims of persecution, borne by countless faithful "in the conviction that the Cross of Christ co-exists with the experience of the Resurrection...the blood of their martyrs known and unknown attaches our Church in a privileged manner to the Age of the Apostles."

Our century has also seen a theological renewal in the areas of patristic studies, liturgical life and icons. Here pioneers have been influential across national frontiers, their universal witness enabling Orthodox theology to be living and present on the international level.

The Primates dealt frankly with the problem of evangelization, in the face of all kinds of sects, and terrifying interpretations of the Apocalypse. Missionary work must be done with humility and "with respect for the freedom and particular character of each one." "The ecumenical movement has given birth to great hope among divided Christians." But there is a warning against the dangers of deviation into "uniatism and proselytism, serious obstacles to progress in our dialogue with Catholics and Protestants."

Two contemporary social problems were singled out for attention: the confusion between freedom and permissiveness, with loss of respect for life; and the threat to the environment, which causes "grave anxiety." The Orthodox Church seeks the adoption of necessary measures for the protection of God's creation and considers man as the organizer, not the owner of natural wealth, "we must give evidence of love and keep an ascetic attitude towards nature." There are some moving reflections on the Eucharist, on the liturgical celebration as the center and criterion of the whole life of the Church. About political issues the policy of non-interference is recalled, save when governments call in question the very existence of Churches. They plead for respect for the international status of Jerusalem and for the Orthodox patriarchate resident there for centuries.

Hoping that the whole world may hear the "voice of faith, hope and love," the Primates conclude thus: "Though the book of the Apocalypse describes dramatic events, it contains the Gospel of Christ, revealing to us that sin and demoniac and destructive forces of man have been and will be conquered by Jesus Christ, the Lord of history, who is the Alpha and the Omega...He who is, who was, who is coming, the Almighty One (Ap. 1:8).

This message was worthy of a very great moment in the history of modern Orthodoxy, a manifestation of renewal, power and hope.

Light from the East

94

Chapter 13

The Holy Land

Bartholomew I's visit to the Holy Land was delayed for some years because of a difficulty arising out of the attitude of Diodoros the Patriarch in regard to certain bishops of the diaspora. When reconciliation was effected, he was happy to enter a region sacred to all Christians, where Orthodox faithful are estimated at about 50,000, slightly less than one third of all the Christian population. He was accompanied by four Metropolitans, Germanos of Tranoupolis, Panteleimon of Belgium, Meliton of Philadelphia and Phillipos of Tyana.[1]

With Diodoros, Bartholomew I went first to the Basilica of the Holy Sepulcher, where a thanksgiving service was celebrated. The Ecumenical Patriarch said that he prayed for peace "everywhere in the world and especially here where the great message of peace was given in the first place here to this Holy Land." On May 13 a working session took place between the two Patriarchs and their assistants; no communiqué was issued.

On May 14 with Diodoros, Bartholomew presided at the Eucharistic liturgy in the Basilica of the Holy Sepulcher, accompanied by several bishops and priests. In his liturgical homily he expressed his esteem and respect for the Patriarchate of Jerusalem: as "guardian of the holy places" it has the task of passing on "the theological and ecclesiological testimony" inherited from the Apostles,

---

[1]   SP., June, 1995.

without which its mission risked to be reduced to the "preservation of simple religious sentiments and historical monuments."

Bartholomew I further developed his thought: "At every liturgical liturgy, the table of sacrifice is for us, Orthodox, at once the grotto of Bethlehem, the Theophany of the Jordan, the Transfiguration on Mount Tabor, the Golgotha, source of our redemption and the tomb from which the general resurrection rises." "Then," he added, "without participation in the Eucharistic experience all these situations remain purely and simply historic monuments with no direct link with true life."

The Patriarch referred to the recent problems between the two Partriarchates, making it quite clear that "the slight little temporary clouds have, in no way, succeeded in covering the clear sky of the relations between our two sister Churches. We support you in your efforts to safeguard the monuments of our faith," he said, speaking directly to the Partriarch Diodoros. "We hope," he continued, "that the union and cooperation of our sister Churches will be strengthened by the grace of the Holy Spirit in the communion of prayer."

Besides the Orthodox in Jerusalem, Bartholomew I met those in Bethany, Jericho, Nazareth, Cana, Tiberias and Mount Tabor. In places he met complaints about indifference towards Arab Orthodox on the part of the Greek prelates; especially they sought to declare their identity and secure protection in a different period. When the Patriarch visited Orthodox monasteries in the Judean desert on May 10, he encountered public protests against his commitment to ecumenism, especially in the direction of Rome.

This unshakable commitment prompted his meetings with the Latin Patriarch, Mgr. Michael Sabah and the Armenian Patriarch, Mgr. Torkom (Manoukian); he urged progress in good inter-relations, while respecting the agreed status quo in regard to use of the holy places by the different communities.

Bartholomew did not shirk contact with the different civil authorities. He was warmly received in Gaza by Yasser Arafat whose wife, Suha Arafat is Orthodox. The leader of the PLO asked the patriarch to take a stand for Palestinian rights, especially in regard to land. He promised his support and his prayers "for the complete application of all the resolutions of UNO, especially in what concerns the Palestinian problem. "The purpose of our visit," he said, "is to assure you that we support you morally." He suggested a pact for Mediterranean peace. While in Gaza, he visited one of the oldest existing churches in the world, Orthodox; its foundation goes back to 410 A.D. About 3,000 Orthodox Palestinians worship there.

On May 15, the Patriarch met Israeli authorities, chief among them the President, Ezer Weizman, and the Prime Minister Yitzhak Rabin. Later in the year, he would hear in Paris of the assassination of this great apostle of peace; with Cardinal Lustiger he would pray publicly for him. So did John Paul II, who also received the dead statesman's widow in audience and consoled her.

Light from the East

Chapter 14

Great Britain

As distinct from previous visits to England, the Patriarch's stay from December 2 to December 8, 1995, was a response to an invitation from Archbishop George Carey of Canterbury, who had visited him at the Phanar in 1994.

This time, Bartholomew I had a heavy program. A reception was given in his honor at Buckingham Palace and another at Lambeth Palace, official residence of the Anglican Primate. He assisted at Vespers in Westminster Abbey and preached there in an ecumenical spirit; he also visited Orthodox communities participating in their liturgies — the Orthodox population is approaching 300,000 with over 200 parishes. All are subject to the Ecumenical Patriarch and have as their Archbishop, Gregorios of Thyateira. He welcomed the Patriarch who was accompanied by Metropolitans Chrysostomos of Ephesus, Meliton of Philadelphia and John of Pergamos. This gave almost a collegial characteristic to the visit, so much probably intended by Bartholomew I. Besides the audience in Buckingham Palace, he had an interview with Sir Nicholas Bosnor, Under-Secretary at the Ministry for Foreign Affairs for Central and Eastern Europe, and attended a reception given in his honor in Leeds Castle by Lord Kingsdow, Lieutenant General for Kent County.

The Patriarch was present at the Sunday office in Cantebury Cathedral, where he prayed on the spot where Tomas Becket was assassinated. Next day he met representatives of the Anglican educational and social services and members of the Anglican Council for Christian unity. Later, he was present at the celebration of Vespers in the Abbey of Westminster; here he spoke on the meaning of asceticism in contemporary society. He spoke still more fully at a reception given in his honor. He spoke of the plans aiming at a strengthening of Orthodox unity and further development of the ecumenical movement in the forthcoming third millennium; he also recalled a subject, we know very well, that is particularly important in his outlook, the protection of the environment; he informed his listeners on the views put forth at the symposium held in Patmos on the nineteenth centenary of the Apocalypse.

There was a working session for the members of the Patriarch's party and the Anglican members of the joint commission for theological dialogue between the Orthodox Church and the Anglican Church. Opening the meeting the Patriarch stated what is for him a fundamental, unquestionable principle: ecumenical dialogue is not an exercise in "ecclesiastical diplomacy" nor "theological work"; it is an obligation in conscience. He could recall former instances of dialogue between different Orthodox Churches and Anglicans, leading to mutual understanding and respect, despite the important theological differences which remain.

Bartholomew I, true to his self-assigned mission, took part in religious ceremonies in Orthodox Churches, in St. Michael's Greek Church in Margate, in the Church of St. Nicholas in Shepherd's Bush — here he assisted at Vespers on the feast day, December 5.

On December 6, the Patriarch celebrated the Eucharistic liturgy in the Greek Cathedral of Santa Sophia at Bayswater. In his homily he spoke of the present situation of the Ecumenical Patriarchate. He was worried about the declining Orthodox numbers in Istanbul. But he took great joy in the fact that Orthodox communities abroad, which are numerically increasing and marked by progress and dynamism, have sought the protection of the Church of Constantinople. He reminded his hearers of the profound meaning of Eucharistic communion — beyond a personal meeting in one spot of Christians living in the same place, it allows us especially to establish "a sacramental union which goes beyond and eliminates geographical distances, and unites all of us in one body, the Body of Christ."

In the afternoon of December 6, Bartholomew I went to Manchester and visited the Greek Orthodox Church of the Annunciation. Next day he was at the Monastery of St. John the Baptist in Maldon, Essex. By a special canonical statute it is directly subject to the Ecumenical Patriarch. He presided at a doxology held in the monastery church, which is dedicated to St. Silouane the Athonite; afterwards he met and conversed with the monks and nuns.

There are altogether over 300,000 Orthodox faithful in Great Britain, mostly but not entirely in the London area, under the jurisdiction of the Archbishop representing the Ecumenical Patriarch, Gregorios of Thyateira. There is also a diocese subject to the Patriarchate of Moscow, ruled by Metropolitan Anthony of Souroge.

Light from the East

Chapter 15

Switzerland and the
World Council of Churches

To end the year 1995, the Patriarch still had important visits to undertake. From December 8 to December 16 he was in Switzerland, where he fulfilled many engagements and, as usual, spoke to great effect before different groups. He was welcomed by Metropolitan Damaskinos, bishop of the diocese of the Ecumenical Patriarchate in Switzerland, and went to celebrate a doxology in the Church of St. Paul, in the Orthodox center of Chambesy. The next day he was received in Berne by the president of the Swiss Confederation, Kaspar Villiger. He was then received by the Old Catholic bishop, and joined in a ceremony in the Cathedral of the Old Catholic Church. On December 10, he presided over the Sunday liturgy in the Orthodox Church of Chambesy. In his homily he referred to pollution and nuclear accidents, asserting that "humanity is threatened by its own creations." He emphasized that the Orthodox Church keeps intact "the authentic continuity of the ancient undivided Church of the East and West," for which reason all Christians could, he claimed, find therein "their common spiritual roots."

On December 11, the Patriarch was the guest of the World Council of Churches. The meeting was given considerable importance by the lengthy address delivered by the Secretary General, Konrad Kaiser. It will bear quotation: "We welcome you as a person who has been linked very closely with the work of the World Council of Churches as a member of the Faith and Order Commission and of the Central Committee. ...How often have you attended ecumenical meetings in this very room and cooperated in our common endeavor to serve Christian unity. This Ecumenical Center is your house, and you have personal roots in Geneva since the days of your studies at the Ecumenical Institute in Bossey during the Graduate School of 1966-67. We appreciate very much that during your visit you will be able to return to Bossey and address the students of the present Graduate School. Among them there might be some future Church leaders, as was the case thirty years ago. We welcome you as the head of an Orthodox member Church, a Church to which the WCC is deeply indebted. According to the testimony of the late Dr. Visser t' Hooft, the encyclical letter sent by the Church in Constantinople in 1920 to 'all the churches in the world' represented the first official proposal by a Church for a permanent instrument of fellowship and cooperation among the Churches. The later founding of the WCC is the fruit of this initiative to create a 'koinonia of churches.' We appreciate the faithfulness of the Ecumenical Patriarchate to the ecumenical movement and the WCC and its perseverance in promoting Christian unity and in furthering cooperation of the theological, ethical and diaconal fields. A tangible evidence of the concern of your Church for the work of the WCC was the creation, exactly forty years ago in 1955, of a Permanent Delegation to the headquarters of the WCC. Over the almost five decades of the existence of the WCC, we have received inspiration and guidance from many bishops, theologians and lay leaders of your Church. The most recent reflection of this shared concern, an initiative with clear ecumenical significance, was your designation of September 1 every year as a day to manifest our Christian calling for the preservation of God's creation. Even if the Ecumenical Patriarchate has criticized some aspects of the WCC from time to time, as was the case with the declaration in 1973 on the occasion of the Council's 25th anniversary, we have always understood that such criticism was intended as a constructive challenge coming from within the fellowship and aiming at a better and more meaningful diaconia of the WCC to the churches and to the world."

What the Secretary General said confirms what has already been clear from our brief review of the outlook and career of Bartholomew I. But it merits reading as a mature appraisal of the prelate and his work. So does Dr. Kaiser's appraisal of the Patriarch's role in the Orthodox Church: "Finally we welcome you as the 'Protos' of the Orthodox church as the *primus inter pares* of the Orthodox episcopate and the symbol of its visible unity. You have repeatedly emphasized the diaconal character of this primacy, and you have demonstrated in the exercise of your leadership that the Church of Constantinople 'does not insist on her own way.' You have given a new expression to this ministry of unity which has been entrusted to you by inviting the heads of all the Orthodox sister Churches for mutual consultation twice since your enthronement. In particular, I wish publicly to recognize here the repeated efforts of your Church to assist Orthodox sister Churches facing existential difficulties even while your own Church has been hard pressed. Your clear commitment to preserving Orthodox unity at the same time is a service to the entire ecumenical movement."

Dr. Kaiser then explained at length three issues or concerns which the WCC wished to discuss with the Patriarch. One was the very fundamental understanding and vision of the WCC. The Secretary General recalled the contribution of an Orthodox member of the founding generation, Metropolitan Germanos of Thyateira, principal author of the 1920 encyclical, continuing to communicate his vision. But now "some (Orthodox) even regard the ecumenical movement with suspicion and consider Orthodox participation in it a betrayal of the true faith." "How can we express in a relevant way the contemporary understanding of the WCC and renew our ecumenical vision as we move into the 21st century?"

Secondly, WCC wished to discuss the "question of communion in the common baptism." "We therefore look to you for guidance regarding how the Ecumenical Patriarchate, with the support of eminent theologians, could help us in redefining the meaning of the fellowship of Churches in the WCC on the basis of their oneness in baptism and in rediscovering the central significance of baptismal communion for the search of Christian unity."

Dr. Kaiser then mentioned a third concern, which as he said, refers to the celebration of Easter. He went on, "Since the Nairobi Assembly in 1975, the Ecumenical Patriarchate has been instrumental in helping the WCC to deal with this issue and has taken a number of initiatives among the Orthodox Churches in order to find solutions acceptable to all. We appreciate particularly the contribution of the ad hoc symposium held at the Orthodox Center in Chambesy in 1976, and we believe that its outcome still constitutes a sound basis for our work on this issue today. Of course, we are aware of the practical and pastoral difficulties which have been expressed by some local Orthodox Churches during the pan-Orthodox pre-conciliar process. Nevertheless, we are confident that the Ecumenical Patriarchate might use its wisdom and influence to reopen the debate. It would be a powerful symbol of the growing sense of Christian unity if, at the beginning of twenty-first century, we would inaugurate a common celebration of Easter on the same date in the year 2001, when the eastern and western calendars coincide. We hope to hear from you whether there are ways in which we can cooperate in order to find mutually-acceptable solutions to this aspiration of the Christian people, particularly in countries where churches of the eastern and western tradition live as close neighbors."

The Secretary General also stated that they wished to consult the Patriarch about relationships between the WCC and its Eastern Orthodox member churches. "You have underlined," said Dr. Kaiser to the Patriarch, "on many occasions that the Orthodox Churches of Constantinople, Cyprus and Greece were founding members of the WCC" from 1961 the entire Eastern Orthodox family had joined. There had been difficulties, and what was found difficult to accept was the "negative attitude if not hostility of some of the Orthodox member churches today." They had tried to meet most of the desiderata and found it difficult to hear of criticisms calling into question the very integrity of the WCC. Clearly the Secretary General was looking to Bartholomew I to effect the necessary harmony.

While in Switzerland, the Patriarch addressed the conference of Swiss bishops. Before them he insisted on the conciliar approach to doctrinal statements and went on to make an assertion which puzzled — if it did not shock some of them, that nowhere in the New Testament is it shown that Peter had authority over the other Apostles. This is traditional Orthodox theology.

Chapter 16

Australia

It is estimated that the Orthodox population in Australia is near the million mark. Bartholomew I, true to his universal pastoral program, undertook a lengthy visitation of the dioceses where they are found; altogether with a visit to New Zealand he spent from November 7 through November 27, 1996, in the area.[1] Everywhere he was welcomed by enthusiastic members of the Orthodox Church; everywhere he was given the highest honors by the civilian authorities. Bartholomew I was accompanied by Metropolitans Constantinos of Derka, Meliton of Philadelphia and Athanasios of Helioupolis.

The outward journey was broken by a stay of two days in Hong Kong. On November 4 the Patriarch gave a lecture in the Chinese University of Hong Kong. In a meeting with the governor, Chris Patten, he spoke of establishing in Hong Kong the seat of an Orthodox diocese for South East Asia; he laid the foundation stone for the cathedral of this diocese. Next day he went to a school for handicapped children and took part, in the Anglican Cathedral of St. John the Evangelist, in an ecumenical ceremony which brought together representatives of the different Christian communities of the city.

On November 7, Bartholomew I arrived in Perth, where he was welcomed by the Australian Prime Minister John Howard and

---

[1] SP., January, 1997.

Archbishop Stylianos, head of the Orthodox Church in Australia. He visited the two Greek Orthodox churches in the city and met the state Prime Minister, Richard Court and the Mayor of Perth, Peter Nattras. When he reached Adelaide on November 9, he was met by a delegation led by the state governor, Sir Eric Neil, who solemnly offered him the keys of the city. He was moved to tears by the immense crowd that welcomed him. He presided at a Sunday Eucharistic liturgy and the next day the Southern University of Australia awarded him a doctorate *honoris causa*.

In Canberra, the federal capital, which Bartholomew I reached on November 12, he had talks with the Prime Minister, John Howard and the Governor General of Australia, Sir William Dean. At an official reception in his honor, the Prime Minister spoke of the "dynamic presence" of the Orthodox community in Australia "which brings a contribution to the Australian nation" especially by means of its educational and charitable works. Replying, the Patriarch extolled cultural pluralism, toleration, dialogue between communities and religions; he felt strongly that the solution to these problems in Australia was important because this is not a country but a continent. Before leaving for a four-day visit to Melbourne, the Patriarch presided over a Eucharistic liturgy on November 13, feast of St. John Chrysostom, in the Church of St. Dimitri.

Again, the civic authorities honored the Patriarch. He was received by the Governor of the State of Victoria, Sir Richard MacGarvie, the Prime Minister, Jeff Kennett, and the city mayor, Ian Deverson. He visited Greek parishes, schools and retreat houses. The highlight was Sunday liturgy in the Melbourne Park Center, before thousands. That was on November 17. The next day after a short stay in Brisbane to preside over a Doxology in the Town Hall, he flew to Wellington in New Zealand. He was received by a Metropolitan Dionysios, whose diocese extends to Indonesia, the Philippines and Korea. Besides visiting the Orthodox parishes, Bartholomew I, on November 20, presided at first Vespers of the Presentation of the Mother of God in the Temple, in St. Andrew's Church. The next day there was a service of ecumenical prayer in the Church of the Annunciation.

The last six days were spent in Sydney. Besides visiting Orthodox parishes, Bartholomew I was received in St. Andrew's Institute of Orthodox Theology, St. Spyridon's College in Kingsford, and St. Euphemia's College in Bankstown, the Vasileias Center of Gerontology, and the Estia Foundation, a retreat house and school for handicapped children. The Prime Minister, Bob Carr, was with the Patriarch at the school for handicapped children; he promised $300,000 for the work. The Patriarch presided over an open-air Eucharistic liturgy on November 24; the attendance was reckoned to be about 17,000. The next day he also presided over a liturgy for the feast of the Archbishop, St. Stylianos, then met members of the National Council of Churches in Australia, Anglicans, Catholics and Orthodox. He went for a trip in the Bay of Sydney with two hundred members of the Australian Orthodox Youth.

Light from the East

Chapter 17

The United States

With characteristic energy and zeal, Bartholomew I devoted practically a whole month to his first visitation of Orthodox centers in the United States. Begun on October 19, 1997, it lasted until November 17. The occasion was the seventy-fifth anniversary of the foundation of the Greek Orthodox Archdiocese in the United States; it was the first visit of the Ecumenical Patriarch since Dimitrios I went in 1990, when he was accompanied by Bartholomew, then his close associate. This time Bartholomew I, after Washington and New York, went to Baltimore, Boston, Atlanta, Chicago, Des Moines, Dallas, San Francisco, Los Angeles, Santa Barbara, Florence, Pittsburgh, and Johnstown. The distinguished visitor delivered more than a hundred addresses. Three themes recurred in these pronouncements: maintenance of the links with the Ecumenical Patriarchate; preservation of the Greek cultural traditions; rejection of secularized society, of which the model — this he asserted more than once, is opposed to the spiritual values of Orthodoxy.

Bartholomew I was received by the highest civic dignitaries: in Washington by President and Mrs. Clinton, by Vice-President Al Gore, Secretary of State, Madeleine Albright, and members of the Senate and Congress; he was the recipient of the Congressional Gold Medal. In New York, the Patriarch was welcomed by the Governor, George Pataki and the Mayor, Rudolph Guliani.

The scholarly world was not lacking in appreciation of one who had not shirked the rigorous demands of academic recognition. The Patriarch was honored with a Doctorate, *honoris causa*, on five occasions: by the universities or higher institutes of Georgetown, Holy Cross Brookline, Tufts Boston, Methodist of the Southern States, and St. Vladimir's.

There was a marked inter-faith note struck in the patriarchal visit. Bartholomew I, shortly after his arrival, visited the United States Holocaust Memorial Museum in Washington where he denounced the culpable attitude of Christians, through their silence, during this terrible catastrophe; he expressed the hope that the "silence during the terrible darkness of the night of Auschwitz" would never again occur. At the Catholic University of Georgetown he took part in a Catholic-Muslim symposium. He also visited Cardinal William Keeler who received him in the oldest Baltimore Catholic Cathedral of the Annunciation in the United States; and also Cardinal Law of Boston. He took part in a number of other ecumenical services. He honored the memory of Martin Luther King in Atlanta and at Santa Barbara presided over the opening of a symposium on *Religion, Science and the Protection of the Environment*, in the presence of Bruce Babbitt, Secretary for the Interior.

There were two highlights in the patriarchal tour of American cities. On November 2, the sixth anniversary of Bartholomew I's inauguration, he celebrated a Eucharistic liturgy accompanied by twelve bishops and a hundred priests in the Navy Pier Palace, Chicago. He spoke afterwards in Greek and, to the young people, in English; as to the young people who had come to listen to him the evening before, numbering 6,000.

While in New York, the Patriarch celebrated a Eucharistic liturgy in Madison Square Garden, in the presence of tens of thousands of the faithful. On the next day, October 27, he addressed the General Assembly of the United Nations and was then the guest of a reception in his honor hosted by the Secretary General, Kofi Annan.

On two questions, the Patriarch's attitude gave reason for surprise. Of the five million Orthodox Christians in the United States, only one and one-half million belong to the Ecumenical Patriarchate; the others are in what Dimitrios, Bartholomew's predecessor, styled "fragmentation." The Patriarch did not refer to this situation; he did not call, as some expected, for a program of unity among the Orthodox. The American press had given considerable attention to the problem before his arrival.

To some observers still more surprising was his opinion on the possible reunion between Orthodox and Catholics. I quote Larry Witham from *The Washington Times*: "The spiritual leader of 250 million Orthodox worldwide addressed a Georgetown University audience after receiving an honorary degree, saying that the East-West split in Christianity cuts to the essence of a human being, what he called 'ontology.' 'The manner in which we exist has become ontologically different,' said Patriarch Bartholomew. 'Unless our ontological transfiguration and transformation toward one common model of life is achieved...unity and its accompanying realization become impossible.'

'The difference,' he suggested, 'was Orthodoxy's more 'mystical' view of life and tradition, which scholars have said does not mesh with the legal and rational approach of western Christianity.' The brief address is considered the most significant inter-Christian statement of the Patriarch's one-month United States visit. It was billed as his public response to Pope John Paul II's letter on the Eastern Church in 1995... 'Our love toward you is warm' Patriarch Bartholomew said to his mostly Catholic audience. He spoke of 'the steadfastness of the Orthodox Church on ecclesiastical assumptions of every type,' referring to the daily life, lines of authority and sources of doctrine. But he said something 'deeper and more substantive' than geography, authority and jurisdictions keeps the churches apart as 'our heart requires that we seek again our common foundations.'"

The tension between the Patriarch and the Holy See was apparent in June 1997 when for the first time in twenty years, a delegation was not sent to Rome for the feast of Saints Peter and Paul. When John Paul II sent a delegation to Istanbul for the feast of St. Andrew, it was received by Bartholomew I who spoke in terms similar to those he used in the United States. "The Orthodox Church," he said, "had the firm conviction that dialogue constitutes the only means of communication, of understanding and mutual exchanges, while taking into account that such a step first demands, on one side and the other, auto-analysis to discover what, on each side, is an obstacle to unity." "It is our responsibility to understand why the object of our desire is still not realized," he declared. He thought that the obstacles did not arise from canonical or ethical questions." It is not a question of disagreements bearing on dogma or the organization of the Church; they are more profound, ontological. "The essential question is this: On the road you follow...have you met Christ and how have you recognized Him? If the answer is yes, then describe Him to me and point out the way. If the answer is no, then tell me why. For my part I would speak to you of my own experience, so that we can help one another as we walk on this road, one leading the other toward Christ, God and man."

"It is possible for us to exchange viewpoints on many other subjects. But even if all these matters were settled, unity would not be fixed among us, if we do not reach agreement on the one Person who is the Head of the Body in which we aspire to be incorporated." He emphasized the reality that the Holy Spirit is the only way that leads to unity in which he finds himself in complete unity with John Paul II.[1] Those who long for Christian unity and pray for its accomplishment will take heart from these words, which manifest a most promising meeting of minds. A reproach at times made to Catholics by the Orthodox concerns the Holy Spirit. It was made in resounding terms in the pages of the *Ecumenical Review* in an article by its editor, a Greek theologian, Nikos Nissiotis, also one time head of the Bossey Institute. He said, in effect, that if the fathers of Vatican II did not say more about the Holy Spirit in their documents, these would have no effect in the Orthodox world.

There would be much to say as commentary on these Orthodox reactions to Catholic teaching. The Doctrine of the Mystical Body of Christ, to which Bartholomew I referred, has been expounded in immense theological literature by Catholics, as it was solemnly taught by Pius XII in an epoch-making Encyclical, *Mystici Corporis Christi*. As to the Holy Spirit, no Pope or Patriarch in history has given such abundant, enlightened teaching on the Third Divine Person as John Paul II. An anthology which I hope to publish will establish this fact beyond a shadow of a doubt.

---

[1] S.O.R.P., 223, 1997.

Chapter 18

The Russian Orthodox Church

The Ecumenical Patriarch, Bartholomew I, is recognized as *primus inter pares*, first among equals, in the Orthodox Church. As we have seen there are several partriarchates. One inevitably attracts much attention, the Russian, rooted in czarist history, marked by the Marxist experience, now rejoicing in freedom. It cannot claim the warrant of antiquity and centuries old widespread acceptance which are the inheritance of Constantinople. But consciousness of vastly numerical superiority in its following, perhaps fifty million to less than five thousand in Constantinople, may have tempted a challenge to the supremacy of the ancient See, as supremacy is understood in the Orthodox world. Any such threat was mastered by the great Athenagoras I.

There have been moments of tension, one of which in regard to Estonia has been mentioned. Another centers on the complex situation in the Ukraine. Bartholomew I had made a visit to Moscow in July 1993. A meeting between him and Alexei II, Patriarch of Russia had been arranged to take place near Vienna before the Second International Ecumenical Congress in Graz, in June 1997; it was canceled.

It is a joy then to narrate the meeting of the two Patriarchs in Odessa on September 24, 1997. The encounter was rendered possible by the arrival in the city of the ship carrying the members of a symposium ecological in character, on *Religion, Science and Environment: The Black Sea in Danger*; the symposium was under the patronage of the Ecumenical Patriarch and the president of the European Commission, Jacques Santer; it was composed of some 250 experts, representatives of different religious communions, theologians, scientists, politicians. At the same time, Alexei II was making a pastoral visit to Odessa.

A joint statement issued after the meeting, which lasted two hours, emphasized the "fraternal character" and the "fruitful results" of the event. Both Patriarchs thought that problems which may arise should be settled as quickly as possible. They intended to maintain contact, either by personal encounters or by telephone.

Chapter 19

Academic Honors

In 1996, on February 2, an honorary doctorate conferred on Bartholomew was given a European dimension. The university was the Flemish Catholic one of Leuven (Louvain), not far from the administrative capital of Europe. A great European figure, Chancellor Helmut Kohl, was similarly honored that day as were representatives of two great universities, Professor Allen Dwek, director of the Institute of Glycobiology in Oxford, and Professor Gerardus 'T Hooft in the University of Utrecht.

The day began with Mass celebrated under the presidency of Cardinal Godfried Danneels, Archbishop of Malines-Brussels, Chancellor of the University, assisted by the four other bishops of Flemish dioceses. The Patriarch was accompanied by Metropolitan Joachim of Chalcedon, Metropolitan Cyril of Gortini (Crete), and Metropolitans Panteleimon of Belgium and Jeremie of France.

The homily was given by Bartholomew I. He raised the question which, as he said, has been long posed: the relations between faith and knowledge. He dwelt on certain ecclesiastics who had contributed to science, citing at length Abbe Georges Lemaitre, a Belgian specialist in astrophysics, Leuven professor, and author of the theory of the "primitive atom," and Fr. Teilhard de Chardin; they could overcome the apparent contradiction between religion and science. "We believe," he said, "that it is important for the unity of Europe to leave behind the virulent polemics of former times between 'believers' and 'non-believers,' polemics often given sustenance by old-time oppositions between 'religion' and 'science,' due to a wrong understanding of one and the other."

Europe, Bartholomew I thought, was searching for its soul — how right he was. The first duty then is to mobilize the intellectual resources of scientists, the political sense of leaders and "the spiritual service of the Church," so that the dynamics of Europe may develop. The Patriarch invited the West to reflect on the Byzantine experience; here was effected the first synthesis between Christianity and Greco-Roman civilization.

Bartholomew I stated his resolute commitment to the unity of the Churches which answers the commandment of Christ "that all may be one," and his firm conviction that without the establishment of "harmonious relations" between the Churches, the unity of Europe will remain "inevitably precarious." "Besides," he added, "we believe that the process of constructing Europe must not under-estimate the dynamics of the Orthodox East, if it really aims at achieving a durable and plenary union."

At the conferring ceremony, Professor J. Delobel stressed the fact that Bartholomew I's principal concern was "to build bridges," after the model of ancient Byzantine, which linked two continents. "The first of these bridges," he said, "is to link the different Orthodox Churches. It is true that as Roman Catholics, we at times envy the mutual independence of the Orthodox Churches, though it is difficult to maintain a balance between Christian unity and lawful pluralism." He thought that the "second bridge" was symbolized by the Patriarch's vigorous call in support of the opening of the European union to the countries of central and eastern Europe. Finally, the third bridge aims at facilitating dialogue between Christians. "The fact," said the Professor, "that he is himself this bridge is the principal reason that influenced the Catholic University of Leuven in its decision to pay homage to the Patriarch Bartholomew I, on this unique occasion."

When, some time previously, on May 31, 1994, Bartholomew I had received an honorary doctorate from London City University, on its centenary, he spoke in St. Paul's Cathedral where the ceremony took place. This time too he was not content with platitudes, as are sometimes the menu on such occasions. He was encouraged by the presence of the Archbishop of Canterbury, the

Bishop of London, and representatives of the political, diplomatic and scientific worlds, notably Prince Philip.

The theme of the Patriarch's address was this time the problems of the city in modern society, with children abandoned to street battles. "The Greeks of ancient times believed," he said "that men could realize their fullest potential in the city...but today we see more and more in our cities the darkest face of life: children with no clothes, food or a roof; people unemployed; brothers killing brothers; broken families, broken lives, broken dreams. We ask ourselves: how can it happen? Our first reaction is not to trust the wisdom of the ancients, but on better reflection one should believe more in it, for if we believe that cities give greater possibilities we shall be led to understand why so many people do not find these possibilities." The answer is in faith. "Knowledge develops the intellect, but faith can open the heart. Wealth builds houses, but faith can move mountains. Politics does what is possible, but faith is capable of the impossible."

Anthropocentric ideologies have failed, the Patriarch thought. Alone politicians, scientists, and university folk cannot resolve the problems facing western civilization: pornography, drugs, poverty, criminality, and the homeless. Here, in the city, the mission of the Church is more vital than ever. "Religious authorities have an essential role; they must manifest the spiritual principles of brotherhood, toleration, morality and renewal — the spirituality of the Church opens the way to realizing possibilities other than those offered by the secularism of the modern world, but they are not necessarily in contradiction. We must urgently counter the effects of secularist humanism by developing the teaching of the Church on man and the world...we must repair the torn fabric of society, calling to mind each day that the misfortune of some among us affects the prosperity of all."

Chapter 20

The Rome Meeting

I

"Blessed is He who comes in the name of the Lord."
(Ps. 118:26)

Your Holiness,

Beloved brothers accompanying the Ecumenical
Patriarch as he visits the Church of Rome. With a deep
sense of personal gratitude, I am pleased to offer you
my most cordial and fraternal welcome. I am particularly grateful because your desired and appreciated visit
enriches with joy the solemnity of Saints Peter and Paul,
the first of the patron saints of the Church of Christ which
is in Rome.

"Behold how good and pleasant it is when brothers dwell
in unity." (Ps. 133:1)

The meeting of brothers in mutual love cannot fail
to produce a deep spiritual resonance in each one. Indeed, brothers experience the grace of common gifts
and feel the Lord's mysterious presence: "For where
two or three are gathered in my name, there I am in the
midst of them." (Mt. 18:20).

Your Holiness, it is my intention to greet in your person, and in those who have accompanied you, the Holy Synod of the Ecumenical Patriarchate and all the Orthodox of the world. I feel that your presence is an expression of the Orthodox Church's very rich spiritual heritage and variety of gifts. In our time, following the great upheavals of recent years, the Orthodox Churches have been committed to reorganizing their pastoral life and their work of evangelization. They can be assured of our sympathy and our readiness to collaborate in the service of proclaiming the one Gospel.

Thus, Pope John Paul spoke as he received Bartholomew I in Rome on June, 1997. This year, instead of the annual delegation sent from Istanbul, it was the Patriarch who came personally. This he had announced. As we have seen he had in the previous year made an exceptional gesture, manifesting unity in prayer with the Pope; he had composed the prayers which the Pope recited at each Station of the Cross on Good Friday. The Pope, in his Apostolic Letter, *Lumen Orientale,* quoted from his own concluding meditation that day.

In the second Encyclical, *Ut Sum Sint*, John Paul recalled his previous personal encounters with a Patriarch of Constantinople: "And how could I ever forget my participation in the Eucharistic liturgy in the Church of St. George, in the Ecumenical Patriarchate, on November 30, 1979, and the celebration in St. Peter's Basilica, on December 6, 1987, in the course of the visit to Rome of my revered friend, Patriarch Dimitrios I? On this occasion, at the Altar of the Confession, we professed the Creed of Nicaea-Constantinople, following the original Greek text."

The stage was set for an historic encounter. This was the third visit to Rome of a Patriarch of Constantinople within thirty years; this was the first Pope in history to welcome to the Eternal City two successive Patriarchs. The event was narrowly to escape an obstacle which threatened some serious embarrassment. On the eve of the feast of Saints Peter and Paul, the Patriarch learned that among a number of archbishops of whom the Pope would confer the pallium during the Mass in St. Peter's would be Archbishop Judson Michael Procyk of Pittsburgh, Metropolitan of the Eastern Byzantine (Ruthenian) Catholics, who number some 250,000 in four dioceses. Tension exists here between Uniates and Orthodox. When the Pope was informed that the Patriarch could not be present at the ceremony, he decided to confer the pallium in this case privately.

The two men meeting at the moment differed, as we have seen. Let us recall how each stood in the discharge of his official duty. Bartholomew I had not yet completed four years in the patriarchate, but in this short period of time he had made a tremendous impact on the Christian world, among the Orthodox, his own flock, and in diverse Catholic and Protestant communities, as in the secular sphere where there was a readiness to hear Christian testimony.

John Paul II had already lengthy experience of the Supreme Office in the Catholic Church. He was in the seventeenth year of his pontificate — he is now the second longest ruling Pope in the present century, only surpassed in this respect by the great Pius XII. His pontificate has been witness to events of exceptional, if not unprecedented character: the collapse of communism in Russia and eastern Europe which could allow two Russian leaders to visit him in Rome, and allow him to visit the historic centers sealed to western influence by the folly of Yalta; a series of papal pastoral journeys worldwide utterly unique in number and extent; the first assassination attempt on a Pope for centuries; a formal, publicly expressed agreement, equivalent to a Concordat, with the state of Israel; a gigantic effort to remove the obstacles impeding unity between the Catholic and Orthodox Churches; spreading apostasy within the Catholic body; a seething minority within the Catholic Church of hard opposition to the Pope's teaching and directives; the publication of an immense volume of teaching on the Holy Spirit, again unique in any pontificate, more than all that emanated from the high office in its entire history; an equally impressive, continuous flow of doctrine and prayer centered on the one whom Bartholomew, himself splendid in this regard, would call *Theotokos*.

Never, in the course of history, have two Christian leaders of such quality and achievement, met.

II

The Patriarch's Homily

Pope John Paul II introduced Bartholomew I, who preached first after the Gospel, with these words:

Dear Brothers and Sisters,

We have just heard the Gospel proclaimed in Latin and Greek as a sign of the universality of the Church, which is invited by the Lord to proclaim the Good News to all nations.

This one Word of God has gathered us here together today to pray for the restoration of full communion between Catholics and Orthodox. With deep joy I urge you to listen to the words of the Ecumenical Patriarch, His Holiness Bartholomew I, my brother in Christ."

Then the Patriarch spoke.

Your Holiness,

The grace of the Holy Spirit, whose supreme triumph the Church experienced in history through Pentecost — celebrated once again in a similar way a few weeks ago in both our liturgical traditions — has gathered us together today in this historic Basilica of St. Peter, in order to glorify, also with spiritual hymns, the God of power and mercy who out of His extreme love for mankind makes possible all that is happening around us, especially this fraternal meeting of ours.

The fact that for years we have met through one another's official delegations on the feasts of each of our Church's patrons is undoubtedly a privilege but at the same a trial since, because of our continuing division, we have not been made worthy yet to receive the grace of the common cup to which, nevertheless, all

Christians who seek and profess the Lord in the East and West, in the North and in the South, continue ardently to aspire.

At this sacred moment we are relishing to a greater degree the spiritual purification of this privilege but also of this trial, as we meet this year personally, to celebrate the venerable memory of Peter, the coryphaeus of the Apostles and Paul, martyred together with Peter in the same Gospel truth and in the same blood of martyrdom.

The first and fundamental matter for Christ, which cannot be repressed, concealed or, even less, abolished by any worldly factor, is without doubt the profession of our immaculate faith, *delivered once for all to the saints* (Jude 1:3), and the obedience which, throughout history *corresponds to and is in conformity* with this irreformable faith.

The apostolic saying, *"Because I believed, I spoke out"* (2 Cor 4:13) is neither rhetorical self-satisfaction nor justification. It is a *law* of life and *a measure of truth* in the Church. Fortunately, theology in the East and in the West has for a long time pointed out, even through contemporary Protestant theologians, that *"Just as Christ is always proclaimed Lord, so faith, at the same time, is always obedience.* (E. Brunner, *Dogmatik* III, p. 59).

For this reason all the Church's vicissitudes — whether they come from without or within, due to our sins — which occur every so often in history, refer, directly or indirectly, to the profession of and obedience to the faith. Hence all the persecutions of the world's faithful; hence also the heresies and disagreements among the faithful.

It is therefore reasonable and proper, at this time and at this historical moment, not merely to call to mind but rather to our consciences and to those of all around us, near and far, the indispensable, indissoluble unity between *the profession of the lips* and the deepest *spirit* for this very *substance* of the faith. We are, moreover, reminded of this now more than ever by the Gospel reading we have just heard about Peter's profession at Caeserea Philippi.

The unparalleled importance of this verse has been recalled more than enough, as everyone knows, by exegetical or polemical theology, in the attempt to identify or to interpret the primacy sought among the Apostles.

Today fortunately, with God's help, we have reached — through many afflictions and humiliations — the maturity of true *apostolic awareness* that is in seeking primacy, not among persons, but rather *among ministries of service*. And we know how many urgent ministries of service face us in the world at every moment, if we are truly concerned not with being "*admired by men*," but with "*being pleasing to God*."

Today when we are learning once again that the principal and queen of Christian virtues, the only one that can truly make the world wise and save it, is *humility* together with *repentance*. This is the most courageous virtue and therefore the most convincing profession of faith. It is not possible to believe and truly profess that "You alone are the Holy One, You alone are the Lord, You alone are the Most High, Jesus Christ, with the Holy Spirit in the Glory of God the Father," and to seek other *powers* and other *glory* in the Church.

Thus great humility and constant repentance as *pastors* and as *flocks* are truly necessary. Even among the faithful, it is not easy to root out the spirit of the world or to be rid of it. In order for us to be worth of having the "*mind of Christ*," we must first reach "*the measure of the stature of the fullness of Christ*" (Eph. 4:13). If, according to the undenied words of the Lord, "*the whole world is in the power of the evil one*" (1 Jn. 5:19), we should also remember the Lord's verdict about him, that is "*this kind cannot be driven out by anything but prayer and fasting*" (Mt. 9:29).

Only with these "*spiritual coordinates*" is the *integrity of the faith preserved in history*, and only then can our faith truly be professed and honored as the power that "overcomes the world." (1 Jn. 5:4).

It is obvious that these spiritual coordinates, as *presuppositions* of the integrity of the faith, clearly show that *orthodoxy* without *orthopraxy* is an *intolerable hypocrisy*, but also that theological reflection on *works* and *faith* is sterile academic verbiage.

However, in asserting this, Your Holiness, and you, my other brothers and sisters, I do not at all wish to disturb our mediation on this solemn occasion. It is rather our intention to declare solemnly to the Christian world today, with sincerity and fear of God, our conviction about the need for *self-criticism* and *constant repentance*.

However, what should be sought in the first place, according to the Christian's *self-criticism* and *repentance,* cannot consist in identifying those *who erred first and those who erred last, nor those who erred the most or the least.* This would be a cowardly, worldly inquiry, which the pre-Christian Greek *thiases* considered an inferior occupation for the spiritual man.

Thus the fundamental issue for us is *how by serving our neighbor we may save him, and how, only with him and through him, we will also be made worthy of salvation.*

In this regard, unfortunately, we Christians have misunderstood Paul's golden rule: *"Bear one another's burdens, and so fulfill the law of Christ"* (Gal. 6:2), as a simple *mutual solidarity of a worldly kind.* Thus it was soon necessary for the Neptic Fathers of the East to complete or rather correctly interpret these words of Paul's with the famous *"self-reproach"* they practiced throughout their life. It is truly the only possibility of *"fulfilling the law of Christ."*

Thus, according to the *patristic self-reproach,* all the sins and errors of our brothers and sisters, other than erroneous beliefs and heresies, weigh not on our brethren but on ourselves. I must spontaneously make myself responsible for them without grumbling, if I truly wish my brethren, my wretched self and the world to be saved.

As the God made man became "like us in every way except sin," thus we too should become like our brethren in every way "except heresy."

If, out of great love for men, the Lord who was alone without sin, was able to say of His Disciples to the Father and to us: "And for their sake I consecrate Myself" (Jn. 17:19), how much more must we, wretched men, purify and consecrate ourselves ceaselessly for the world, through our *kenosis*.

Lastly, as we congratulate one another and embrace on this great feast we are celebrating today, may we be allowed to state that truly, only when the primacy of the *kenotic ethos* prevails convincingly in the historical Church, will we not only be able easily to reestablish our deeply desired unity in faith, but we will also make ourselves immediately worthy of experiencing all that God's revelation has promised to those who love the Lord, that is, "a new earth and a new heaven." Amen.

III

The Patriarch's Angelus Reflection

Bartholomew I spoke from the central loggia of St. Peter's Basilica, in the company of Pope John Paul II.

Together we are celebrating the Solemnity of the Apostles. We are celebrating the sacred memory of Peter and Paul. Glory, honor and grace to Holy God for this feast common to both. Our thanks to our brother, the Bishop of Old Rome, His Holiness Pope John Paul II.

An embrace of esteem and love to you all, children of God near and far! The feast of the Apostles and martyrs invites us to deep reflection. It invites us to renew our zeal for the mission and contemporary witness of the Church.

This is what we, the Bishops of Old and New Rome, have accomplished with full awareness. We have remembered with tears the myriads of martyrs of the early Church, who in this city faced wild beasts for Christ's name. The beasts are still alive. They are before us, among us, within us. They are sin, arrogance, lies, deceit, zeal not in accord with a right conscience, fanaticism, divisions, war, fear and death.

Nevertheless, the Lord God of the Apostles and martyrs, our God, lives and we live in Him. He has sent us and still sends us into the world. We go forth, proclaiming reconciliation and unity. We are witnesses to the reflection of Christ. We are not afraid of the beasts, because we have our Comforter, the Holy Spirit, the Spirit of truth, Treasury of all good and Giver of life. Therefore, brothers and sisters, take heart! God loves the world, He loves man, He loves life; let us too love one another in the truth, and the God of love, peace and unity will be with us always. Amen.

IV

The Common Declaration

This was signed on the evening of Thursday, June 29, at the last meeting of the Pope and the Patriarch in the Vatican, before Bartholomew's departure.

"Blessed be the God and Father of our Lord Jesus Christ who has blessed us in Christ with every spiritual blessing" (Eph. 1:3).

1. We also thank God for this brotherly meeting of ours which took place in His name and with the firm intention of obeying His will that His disciples be one (Jn. 17:21). Our meeting has followed other important events which have seen our Churches declare their desire to relegate the excommunica-

tions of the past to oblivion, and to set out on the way to re-establishing full communion. Our venerable predecessors, Athenagoras I and Paul VI became Pilgrims to Jerusalem in order to meet in the Lord's name, precisely where the Lord, by His Death and Resurrection, brought humanity forgiveness and salvation. Subsequently their meetings at the Phanar and in Rome have initiated this new tradition of fraternal visits in order to foster a true dialogue of charity and truth. This exchange of visits was repeated during the ministry of Patriarch Dimitrios, when, among other things, the theological dialogue was formally opened. Our new-found brotherhood in the name of the one Lord has led us to frank discussion, a dialogue that seeks understanding and unity.

2. This dialogue — through the Joint International Commission — has proved fruitful and has made substantial progress. A common sacramental conception of the Church has emerged, sustained and passed on in time by the apostolic succession. In our Churches, the apostolic succession is fundamental to the sanctification and unity of the People of God. Considering that in every local Church the mystery of divine love is realized and that is how the Church of Christ shows forth this active presence in each one of them, the Joint Commission has been able to declare that our Churches recognize one another as Sister Churches, responsible for safeguarding the one Church of God, in fidelity to the divine plan, and in an altogether special way with regard to unity.

    We thank the Lord of the Church from the bottom of our hearts because these affirmations we have made together not only hasten the way to solving the existing difficulties, but henceforth enable Catholics and Orthodox to give a common witness to faith.

3. This is particularly appropriate on the eve of the third millennium when, 2,000 years after the birth of Christ, all Christians are preparing to make an examination of conscience on the reality of his proclamation of salvation in history and among men.

    We will celebrate this Great Jubilee on our pilgrimage towards full unity and towards that blessed day, which we pray is not far off, when we will be able to share the same bread and the same cup in the one Eucharist of the Lord.

    Let us invite our faithful to make this spiritual pilgrimage together towards the Jubilee. Reflection, prayer, dialogue, reciprocal forgiveness and mutual fraternal love will bring us closer to the Lord and will help us to better understand His will for the Church and for humanity.

4. In this perspective we urge our faithful, Catholics and Orthodox, to reinforce the spirit of brotherhood which stems from the one Baptism and from participation in the sacramental life. In the course of history and in the more recent past, there have been attacks and acts of oppression on both sides. As we prepare, on this occasion, to ask the Lord for His great mercy, we invite all to forgive one another and to express a firm will that a new relationship of brotherhood and active collaboration will be established.

    Such spirit should encourage both Catholics and Orthodox, especially where they live side by side, to a more intense collaboration in the cultural, spiritual, pastoral, educational and social fields, avoiding any temptation to undue zeal for their own community to the disadvantage of the other. May the good of Christ's Church always prevail. Mutual support and the exchange of gifts can only make pastoral activity itself more effective and our witness to the Gospel we desire to proclaim more transparent.

5. We maintain that a more active and concerted collaboration will also facilitate the Church's influence in promoting peace and justice in situations of political or ethnic conflict. The Christian faith has unprecedented possibilities for solving humanity's tensions and enmity.

6. In meeting one another, the Pope of Rome and the Ecumenical Patriarch have prayed for the unity of all Christians. In their prayers they have included all the Baptized who are incorporated into Christ, and they have asked for an ever deeper fidelity to the Gospel for the various communities.

7. They have in their heart a concern for all humanity, without any discrimination according to race, color, language ideology or religion.

   They therefore encourage dialogue not only between the Christian Churches, but also with the various religions, and above all, with those that are monotheistic.

   All this doubtless represents a contribution and a presupposition for strengthening peace in the world, for which our Churches pray constantly. In this spirit we declare, without hesitation, that we are in favor of harmony among peoples and their collaboration, especially in what concerns us most directly. We pray for the full realization of the European union, without delay, and we hope that its borders will be extended to the East.

   At the same time we make an appeal that everyone will make a determined effort to solve the burning problem of ecology, in order to avoid the great risk of threatening the world today, due to the abuse of resources that are God's gift.

   May the Lord heal the wounds tormenting humanity today and hear our prayers and those of our faithful for peace in our Churches and in all the world.

V

The Patriarch made a number of important visits while in the Eternal City. He paid a warm courtesy call on his former College, the French Seminary; he met the professors and students of the Lateran University. We shall delay on his homily preached in St. Peter's and on his Angelus reflection on that same feast day. We should see something of what he said on two other occasions.

Bartholomew I addressed formally the members of the Roman Curia. Here, in meeting them, he was probably influenced by the Orthodox practice of government, by synod. He has made it clear, more than once, that the Orthodox Church must persevere in this mode of rule.

Thus he spoke:

> "*Greet one another with the kiss of peace*" recommends the Apostle Peter, proto-coryphaeus (1 Pt. 5:14). "*Let us then pursue what makes for peace and for mutual upbuilding*," the Apostle of the Gentiles exhorts us (Rm. 14:19).
>
> Following Peter and Paul and maintaining a custom already hallowed for years, we and all those with us, have come here with joy at being present for the feast of the patrons of Old Rome, to pursue sincerely, without pretense, the work of peace and mutual edification.
>
> Thus, embracing you fraternally with deep love and esteem, we thank you for your fraternal welcome. We are also grateful for the special joy of having social contact with you, the members of the Roman Curia, and other officials of the group of those who work closely with His Holiness, my beloved brother in Christ and Bishop of Rome, Pope John Paul II.
>
> Brothers, we know or we can imagine the enormity and the burden of your personal and collegial responsibility in the exercise of your lofty duties, just as you will certainly know or at least easily have an idea of our responsibility and that of those who work with us. Over and above the differences in proportion (in quantity and

number) and, to a certain extent, in the type of institutions, we also take for granted that in the last analysis our work like yours, is for God's glory and for the salvation of man and the world. This is the very task to which the Lord called the holy Apostles and Evangelists, the Prophets, Doctors and Pastors of the Church; it is the work to which God continues to call us, distributing the charisms of the Spirit for building up the body and for its growth.

Thus we are deacons of the tremendous mystery of salvation in the Church's perennial Pentecost. But every day we too encounter the *"mystery of iniquity"* (2 Thess. 2:7) which still continues. Iniquity in the overall reality of the contemporary world. Iniquity in the very life of Christians, which is sometimes expressed as errors in matters of faith and at others, as moral corruption, not infrequently giving rise to scandal and justified criticism. But there is also that other iniquity, which each of us has experienced in his own life and, together with St. Paul we ask: "Wretched man that I am! Who will deliver me from this body of death?," which in the form of a confession for himself and as an entreaty for us, he mentions in the seventh chapter of his Letter to the Romans. Particularly those of us who have been honored by God with the dignity of the priesthood have intimate knowledge of this personal struggle, but also of the faithful who are close to us and who unburden themselves of their sorrow and trials to the Church.

For all the reasons mentioned above, it is necessary for us to seek one another's company more regularly in the spirit of St. Paul, who wrote to the Christians in Rome: "I long to see you, that I may impart to you some spiritual gift to strengthen you, that is, that we may be mutually encouraged by each other's faith, both yours and mine."

In this regard, you know that the divine Spirit-bearing Apostles having Christ himself as a model and an example in all things, not only overcame human disagreements but supported one another, among other things, through communion and the exchange of their charisms.

It can be said that this exchange of charisms in the Church's life represents the extension and fruit of the exchange itself of the "idioms" of Christ's two natures, which came about as we were taught, that is, by "each nature exchanging its own idioms with those of the other" (Migne Pg. 77, 1172D). The ancient Church of the Apostles knew, respected and followed this exchange, that is, the interpretation of one with the other. On the one hand she had Christ as model and example, on the other, she knew full well that the visible union sincerely sought once again today may be glimpsed above all "in the exchange of one's own things" (Pg. 86 1176D). In other words, the Church of those times knew that in the mystery of *kenosis* and the Cross, Christ the Lord subjected the human race to God the Father and gave us himself "as a perfect model and example" (Pg. 94, 1076B) so that we too, "being of the same race, may become with one another, one in the Spirit, having as our model the Son's unity of nature with the Father" (Pg. 26, 365A).

In this spirit of our faith, our ethos, our heart and soul, we come to our brother John Paul II and to you all in Rome, ready to celebrate together, that is, to be led together into the depths and to renew our faith and our hope.

Since we both exercise a power that is primarily spiritual, we need for example, to be ever ready to justify ourselves to those who ask us, as they once asked the Apostles: "By what power or by what name did you do this?" (Acts 4:7). Furthermore, we need to understand more deeply, day by day, the mystery of the spiritual, and at the same time, existential experience of Paul the Apostle, who heard the Lord say in His hour of affliction: "My grace is sufficient for you, for my power is made perfect in weakness" (2 Cor. 12:9). Only in the heart of this mystery of weakness and grace can we fight against the evil one and the temptation of power, and humbly accept the divine precept and exhortation: "Whoever would be first among you must be your slave" (Mt. 20:27). Moreover, we have come to receive from your charisms with gratitude, and to offer spontaneously what God has entrusted to us and to our Church in the East. Therefore, we beg you on this festive occasion, and we ask you also for our sake" to supplement your faith with virtue, and virtue with knowledge, and knowledge with self-control, and self-control with steadfastness, and steadfastness with brotherly affection and brotherly affection with love" (2 Pt. 1:5-7). Therefore, receive our kiss and our love, offered from the depth of our heart.

You know that we declared 1995 the Year of Revelation, on the occasion of the fulfillment of 1900 years since John, the divine mystic of Patmos, recorded the revelations made to him in the last book of Sacred Scripture. We call all to listen together with due attention to the words of the prophecy and to observe what is written in it (Rev. 1:2). In a particular way, we call all to listen to "what the Spirit says to the Churches" today (Rev. 2:11): to understand the magnitude of the danger when we are neither hot nor cold but lukewarm (Rev. 3:15-16); to make ourselves aware of God's affliction, since we have abandoned the love we had at first (Rev. 2:4); to identify the contemporary features of the *Beast*; to perceive as our own the groans of our natural environment for all the harm caused to it by the *Destroyer* or *Perdition,* and for what the star called Wormwood threatens (Rev. 8:11), to bring about, while resisting the anguished life caused by loss of the image of heaven from the consciousness of many, their reevangelization with the image of our eschatological expectation, that is, the heavenly Jerusalem, the vision of God's new world, the new earth and the new heaven. It is impossible, we are not permitted to reach the end of the second millennium of Christ and usher in the third by holding up before mankind the image of the *Lamb, as if slain* (Rev. 5:6), among other things, because of our errors and our divisions, due to which the image of the Risen Christ has become blurred for many. On the contrary, bowing in repentance before God and advancing towards *reconciliation* through our renewal in the Holy Spirit, we must bring back to men's eyes the image of the Lamb inviting us all to His wedding feast. This is the only salutary invitation amid the catastrophic provocations of the present time.

This newness, the eschatological perspective of the faithful and the expectation of the Church, is the only and ultimate hope for the whole of humanity. Before it, we, the Old and the New Rome, have a specific responsibility. Let us pray intensely during these feast days of the Apostles, that God may strengthen us in the exercise of this responsibility so that we may respond to his call with humility and faith: "Yes, come Lord Jesus!."

VI

Have the members of the Roman Curia, given to problems of administration, ever heard from a member of another Church, an address so profoundly spiritual? Why did the Patriarch choose to speak at length in such terms to these officials? One may ask similar questions on reading the text of his address to the youth whom he met in the Basilica of Sancta Maria in Transtevere, under the auspices of the Community of St. Egidio. Stating that it was difficult to be "both young and Christian" in a moment of "great changes and numerous challenges" Bartholomew I spoke these enlightening and comforting words:

A moment of great changes and of numerous challenges. We know how difficult it is today to be both young and Christian. Now that Europe is reaching the end of the second millennium in Christ, she at least should be a truly Christian continent. But it is just from

Europe that have come the enemies of Christ par excellence and the persecutors of the children of God. That is what this century which is nearing its end confirms in tragic fashion. Nevertheless, may the name of the Lord be glorified for young people like you who are eager and ready to carry his Cross before those who hate him.

We repeat: the work is great; very great are your mission and your responsibility. And for that we owe you love, honor and thankfulness. We forget this at times, we, the elders, even those who exercise spiritual functions in the Church.

We often declare: young people are the hope of the Church. That is true on condition nonetheless that you are not left on the margin of the Church's life, for you are not only the future, you are also the present. What the Apostle Paul wrote to his disciple, Timothy, who, though young, had taken on great responsibilities in the life of the primitive Church, is always valid: 'Let no one despise you because you are young, but be an example to the faithful in speech, in conduct, in charity, in faith and in chastity." (1 Tim 4:12). What is more promising than to see young Christians, able to be an example for those who are within and especially for those who are outside the Church. The Church is not properly oriented towards the future save when it leaves a free area for the full development and effective exercise of the charisms of all its members, especially the young.

We have already said that it is difficult today to be Christian, but it is also difficult to be young. We must know that life if hard today for young people, how insensitive it is. Instruction becomes daily more demanding, but without giving people genuine education, or guaranteeing a professional future. Constantly rising unemployment restricts your way ahead. Society apparently consoles you with ideas and with drugs. The social communications media frequently wind up as a means of general confusion and deviation.

You are, unfortunately, the AIDS generation, and this new appalling scourge, in addition to its bodily threat, destroys what is purest, most sacred, most profoundly human in life, this very life in the fullness and creativity of love.

But, young friends of Rome, there is still hope. The way is narrow, but there is an exit. In truth this is that to which the experience of the Church for twenty centuries bears witness: experience of crucifixion and resurrection. Faith, love, mercy, pardon, mastery of egoism, truth are found, there too is the light of God which dispels the darkness and reveals the ways of salvation.

We, Orthodox of the East, affirm and confirm this openly. Our oldest and most recent experience bears witness to it. Suffering is great; persecution is hard; poverty is inexorable; experience of death is daily. And with all that? Here we are still living, because the Lord our God is living. Remain faithful to hope, and hope does not disappoint, as St. Paul wrote to your ancestors, the Christians of Rome at that time (cf. Rm. 5:5).

Once again, we thank you for the gift of communion with you. And since this gift had been precious, we expect other gifts from you in the future, of a kind to support us in the struggle. And the gifts we ask of you are those which the Apostle Paul asked for himself from the Christians of Philippi. And we desire to be informed in the future about these gifts from the young people of Rome. And your gift will be our consolation.

St. Paul wrote and we state it with him: 'So then, my brethren, beloved and longed-for, my joy and my crown, stand fast in the Lord... Rejoice in the Lord always... whatever is just and pure... Think upon these things. And the God of peace will be with you' (Ph. 4:1 sq).

All my thanks to you, to you my paternal wishes and the patriarchal blessing which I grant with deep love.

VII

Homily of John Paul II

1. *"You are the Christ, the Son the living God"* (Mt.
    16:16). Today the Church returns to this confession,
    spoken by Peter near Caeserea Philippi. This is *the
    faith of the Apostolic College, in whose name Peter
    is speaking*. This is the faith of Paul. Both Peter and
    Paul bore witness to it even to the shedding of their
    own blood. According to tradition, this happened
    here in Rome in Nero's time, around the year 67
    after the birth of Christ.

    Today, in a particular way, we commemorate
    Andrew, Simon Peter's brother, who was the first to
    be called (*Protokletos*) and who brought Simon to
    Christ. With intense feeling, we call his figure to
    mind today because on this solemn day *the Church
    of Rome welcomes as her guest* Patriarch
    Bartholomew of Constantinople, and the Church
    over which he presides is especially linked to the
    person and martyrdom of the Apostle Andrew.

    Every year on November 30, the Feast of St.
    Andrew, the Church of Rome joins her sister Church
    in honoring her patron. It is a deep joy for us today,
    as we recall the glorious memory of Simon Peter,
    Andrew's brother, to be able to welcome to Rome
    the Ecumenical Patriarch, His Holiness
    Bartholomew I of Constantinople, the first See
    among the world's Orthodox Churches. Today, with
    Andrew, Peter utters these words: "You are the
    Christ, the Son of the living God" (Mt. 16:16).

2. This confession discloses *the mystery of God the
    Father* to us. Christ, in responding to Peter's words,
    said: "Blessed are you, Simon Bar-Jona. For flesh
    and blood has not revealed this to you, but my Fa-
    ther, who is in heaven" (Mt. 16:17). The Father re-

veals the Son because only the Father knows the Son, as only the Son knows the Father (cf. Lk 10:22). The Church professes this faith with the words of the *Nicene-Constantinopolitan Creed: I believe in one God, Father Almighty...*"

This is a venerable text which we both recognize as a normative and irrevocable expression of the Church's one faith. No confession of which belongs to a specific liturgical tradition can contravene such a fundamental expression of the Trinitarian faith, taught and professed by the Church in all ages.

3. In this regard, it is necessary to clear up a misunderstanding which still casts its shadow on relations between Catholic and Orthodox. To this end a Joint Commission was established. Its task is to explain, in the light of our common faith, the legitimate meaning and importance of different traditional expressions concerning the eternal origin of the Holy Spirit in the Trinity, expressions that are part of our mutual doctrinal and liturgical heritages. On the Catholic side, there is a firm desire to clarify the traditional doctrine of the *Filioque*, present in the liturgical version of the Latin *Credo*, in order to highlight its full harmony with what the Ecumenical Council confesses in its creed; the Father as the source of the whole Trinity, the one origin of both the Son and the Holy Spirit.

The Son, consubstantial with the Father, is the *Eternal Word* of which the Apostle John wrote in his prologue to the Fourth Gospel, confessing the Word who "became flesh and dwelt among us" (Jn. 1:14). According to tradition, St. John wrote the Gospel in Ephesus, thereby becoming particularly dear to all the Christian East. His Gospel was the light that illumined the Church throughout the world.

We, the successors of Peter and Andrew, united today in veneration of the holy Apostles Peter and

Paul, would also like to *illumine our meeting with the light of John's Gospel*, so that it may be clear that the same truth about the Father and the Son is professed by us and proclaimed in common.

4.   *"You are the Christ, the Son of the Living God"* (Mt. 16:16). Peter confesses this and, together with him, so does the whole Church which was founded on the Apostles. In confessing Jesus of Nazareth as the Christ, the Church is also indirectly proclaiming the *truth about the Holy Spirit*. In fact the name "Christ" from the Hebrew "Messiah" means one who is anointed with God's Spirit. This truth was expressed by the Prophet Isaiah many centuries before Christ in the words Jesus was to proclaim and bring to fulfillment at the beginning of His Messianic activity: *"The Spirit of the Lord is upon me, because He had anointed me to preach the good news to the poor"* (Lk. 4:18).

The Holy Spirit, whom the Father sends in the name of the Son (cf. Jn. 14:26), has been the source of the Church's life since the day of Pentecost, in accordance with the Redeemer's promise: "He will teach you all things, and bring to your remembrance all that I have said to you" (Jn. 14:26). The Spirit, who guides the Church and teaches her, who consecrates the Bishops as successors of the Apostles, *is with us today in a particular way*, as He was with Peter and Paul on the day of their martyrdom when they bore their definitive witness to Christ and sealed their mission with blood, leaving it as an inheritance not only to Rome, but to so many other places in the ancient world.

And how many of these places are found in Greece! It is enough to list the communities to which St. Paul's Letters are addressed. From the "Pauline corpus," as it were, *a common tradition of the Church in the East and the West* emerges. The whole series of Apostolic Letters in the New Testament are proof of their concern for all the Churches entrusted by God to the Apostles and to their successors until the end of time.

5. "*You are Peter, and on this rock I will build My Church*, and the powers of death shall not prevail against it. I will give you the keys of the kingdom of heaven, and whatever you bind on earth shall be bound in heaven, and whatever you loose on earth shall be loosed in heaven." (Mt. 16:18-19).

These words are overwhelming. *The authority which Christ hands over to the Apostles*, that of the keys of the kingdom of heaven and that of binding and loosing, is given to them in the person of Peter and in union with him. *An unfathomable mystery*.

Today's feast of the martyrdom of the holy Apostles reveals what is the true meaning of authority: *it is service*. Peter, Paul and Andrew served even to the shedding of their blood, just as Christ had done before them: "For the Son of man also came not to be served but to serve, and to give His life as a ransom for many." (Mk. 10:45*). The Apostles were called to participate in their Master's service*: a service by which they were able to give the ultimate testimony; a service that was their true strength, their glory in Christ who died and rose again.

Today we wish to honor those who, in the course of the 2,000 years of the new era, have witnessed and continue to witness to Christ in every corner of the earth, in the East and in the West, in the North and in the South. We would especially like to honor all those who have borne witness to the point of shedding their blood. *We prepared ourselves for today's meeting by pondering again over the paths that this witness took in the Roman Colosseum and in the many other 'colosseums' scattered throughout the world. Last Year's Way of the Cross* was a great help

in this common reflection, whose texts were prepared in fact by our Brother, Bartholomew I.

6. Today's solemn liturgy is enriched by an additional
and meaningful rite, *the imposition of the pallium*.
The pallium, which today the Bishop of Rome con-
fers on the new Metropolitans, is an expression of a
special spiritual bond with the confession and witness of St. Peter in Rome, and with the ministry of
his successor.

I embrace you with affection, beloved Brother
Archbishops, and I rejoice in the fact that, having
been sent to preside over Metropolitan Churches in
various parts of the world, you will receive the pallium in the presence of our guest, the Ecumenical
Patriarch of Constantinople.

7. The solemnity of Saints Peter and Paul invites us to
reflect on the way taken by Peter and Paul as they
followed Christ from the day of their calling to that
of their martyrdom here in Rome. The first reading
from the Acts of the Apostles showed us St. Peter
while he was still in Jerusalem on the first stage of
the Church's long pilgrimage.

We listen together to the words of this passage,
which in a certain sense recounts our own history,
Venerable Brother Bartholomew I. We listen to it in
deep veneration and feeling, *now that the 2000th
year since the birth of Christ is approaching. It represents a great challenge for the whole of humanity
and especially for all Christians*. When I think of
this historic goal, I am reminded of what St. Luke's
Gospel says about the disciples' mission: *He sent
them ahead of Him, two by two*" (Lk. 10:1). We
should meditate on the meaning of these words. Do
they not suggest that *Christ is also sending us two-
by-two as messengers of* His Gospel in the West and
in the East?

VIII

Angelus Mediation of John Paul II
June 29, 1995

Spoken before praying the Angelus after Mass in St. Peter's Basilica in the presence of Patriarch Bartholomew I:

Dear Brothers and Sisters:

1. Today we are celebrating the Solemnity of Saints Peter and Paul, a feast of Rome which venerates them as her patrons; a feast of the whole Church, whose spiritual edifice is founded on these two pillars: the Prince of the Apostles and the Teacher of the Gentiles. Today my joy, which I would like to share with all of you, is even greater because the Church of Rome has the privilege of having as her guest the Ecumenical Patriarch, His Holiness Bartholomew I, together with the venerable Brothers who have accompanied him.

   How can we fail to remember the bonds of affection which unite us? How can we fail to make explicit mention of the fact that last year he prepared the texts for the Good Friday Way of the Cross at the Colosseum? In a certain sense it was an anticipation of today's gift. Here I would like wholeheartedly to renew my greetings to my brothers and sisters of the Orthodox Church, assuring them of the esteem and affection of the entire Catholic Church. Together we are commemorating the wonders worked by the Holy Spirit in our Christian communities since the beginning, since the martyrdom of the First Apostles.

2. Does not our present joyous meeting remind us of the respective patrons of Constantinople and Rome, the brothers, Andrew and Simon? According to the Evangelist John's account, it was precisely Andrew

who introduced his brother to Jesus (cf. Jn. 1:40-42).

From that moment, Andrew and Simon followed Christ together, both sharing death on a cross with him, that cross which Saul of Tarsus, converted on the way to Damascus, was to proclaim to the world as the only reason to boast. Today, looking with the vision of faith at the past two millennia, and the third one now at hand, *together we would like to confess* that Christ alone is the world's salvation. Only his Death and Resurrection represent true liberation from evil and death. His Cross is the force of reconciliation and peace; it forms the basis of hope for believers in every time and place.

We are one in Christ; we are called to proclaim the Gospel of joy and life to the world. Like Andrew, like Peter and Paul, we must all proclaim it with our life and with our words, never ashamed, but glorifying Christ's cross. On the Cross the Redeemer opened his heart to us as the sacrament of the "heart" of God, almighty and merciful, the Creator and Lord of the universe.

3. Mary, Mother of God and of the Church, shared with the Apostles the hour of hardship and the hour of communion with John, she remained faithful beneath the Cross of the Son of God; at Pentecost she welcomed the gift of the Holy Spirit in the Upper Room with the Apostles, sealing by her presence the birth of the Church sent forth to evangelize humanity to the very ends of the earth.

Oh Mary, look down upon the successor of Peter and the successor of Andrew, gathered here today. Grant that the Christians of the East and those of the West will always advance on the way of unity and fidelity to the Gospel. Renew the miracles of the early Christian communities in these years leading up to the year 2000, so that contemporary humanity will believe in Christ, the one Savior of the world.

Note on the Appendices

Appendix I is the text of the Pope's reflections spoken at the conclusion of the Stations of the Cross on Good Friday, 1994, during which he had read the mediation for each Station prepared by Bartholomew I.

Appendix II gives the reaction of Bartholomew I to the Pope's Apostolic Letter, *Orientale Lumen*, on the Orthodox Church.

Appendix III is the memorandum submitted to the World Council of Churches by the Ecumenical Patriarchate in answer to its request for suggestions on its running.

Appendix IV is a brief historical note on the General Councils of the Church accepted by the Orthodox.

Appendix V is the complete text of the most important interfaith agreement, at the level of dialogue by theologians, between Orthodox and Roman Catholics, *The Balamand Declaration*, June 1993. The inter-faith commission responsible for this historic document was established by Dimitrios I and John Paul II; its findings have been welcomed by the Pope in his Encyclical *Ut Unum Sint*.

Appendix VI presents texts of the synodical act of the Patriarchate of Constantinople regarding Estonia and of the letter sent to the Patriarch of Moscow; they are given as an instructive example of the functioning of government in the Orthodox Church: the synodical principle.

John Paul II's Reflections after the Stations of the Cross.

Brothers and Sisters:

1. Today we are here to contemplate the mystery of the mystery of the Cross that we adore in the Good Friday Liturgy; *Ecce lignum Crucis Venite Adoremus.*

    Let us adore him now; here; in the Colosseum. Here where our ancestors in the faith witnessed by their martyrdom even to the point of death, to the love with which Christ loved us. Here in this spot in the globe, in ancient Rome, I am thinking especially of the "Hill of Crosses" in Lithuania, to which I made a pastoral visit last September. I was moved by that other Colosseum, not of distant Roman times but a Colosseum of our age, of the last century.

    Before going to Lithuania in the Baltic lands, I prayed for these two evangelization routes: the one that went from Rome towards the north, east and west; the other that led from Constantinople, from the Oriental Church. These two routes converged precisely there in the Baltic countries, between Lithuania and Russia.

2. Today, the wisdom of the Eastern Tradition has guided us in our meditation of the *Via Crucis* through the words of our beloved Brother Bartholomew, Ecumenical Patriarch of Constantinople. We sincerely thank him.

I thought of those other Colosseums, so numerous, of those other "Hills of Crosses" that are on the other side, throughout European Russian, throughout Siberia, so many "Hills of Crosses," so many Colosseums of modern times.

Today I would like to say to my brother from Constantinople, and to all our Eastern brothers and sisters; "Dearly beloved, we are united in these martyrs from Rome, from the "Hill of Crosses, the Solvietsky Islands and many other extermination camps. We are united against the background of these martyrs, we cannot fail to be united.

We cannot fail to speak the same truth about the Cross and why should we not say it? Because the world today is seeking to empty the Cross of its power. This is the anti-Christian tradition that has spread for centuries and wants to empty the Cross of its power. It wants to tell us that man is not rooted in the Cross, nor has even the prospects of the Cross or hope in it. Man is only human, he must live as though God did not exist.

3. Dearly beloved, we have this common task, together from East and West we must say: *Ne evacuetur Crux!* The Cross of Christ must not be emptied of its power because if the Cross of Christ is emptied of its power, man no longer has roots, he no longer has prospects: he is destroyed!

    This is the cry of the twentieth century. It is the cry of Rome, of Moscow, of Constantinople. It is the cry of all Christendom, of the Americas, of Africa, or Asia, of everyone. It is the cry of the new evangelization.

    Jesus tells us: they have persecuted me, they will persecute you too; they have listened to me, they have received My Word, they will receive yours also. They will receive it, they have no other solution. No one has words of eternal life, only he has, only Jesus, His Cross alone.

    Therefore, at the end of this *Via Crucis* in our ancient Roman Colosseum, we think of all the other Colosseums and we greet them in love, in faith, in common hope.

4. Let us entrust ourselves, the whole Church and all humanity to this Mother who stands beneath the Cross and embraces us all

like children. In her love, we, like John feel the strength of this unity, this communion of the Church and of Christianity and we give thanks to the Father, the Son and the Holy Spirit for Christ's Cross.

Praise be Jesus Christ!

Happy Easter![1]

---

[1] ORE, April 6, 1994.

Light from the East

The Patriarch
and *Orientale Lumen*

Bartholomew I gave an interview to the Italian periodical *Il Regno* on the Pope's Apostolic Letter *Orientale Lumen*. The interview appeared on June 15, just twelve days before the Rome meeting of the Pope and the Patriarch; the letter had been published on the preceding May 3. Though the papal document was dated for the centenary of Leo XIII's Apostolic Letter *Orientalium Dignitas*, and bore no allusion to the imminent meeting, the Patriarch welcomed it and noted that it was designed to stir knowledge and appreciation of the spiritual values of the Christian Orient, study and re-evaluation of them by Christians of the West, in view of the reunion which both desire. Bartholomew I rejoiced in the papal recognition of the glorious elements in Orthodoxy, monasticism, worship, apophatism of its theology, the patristic treasures of the first millennium of Christianity lived together, when the orthodox Orient was par excellence the decisive factor of theological principles and cultural values for the whole of Christianity.

The Patriarch had "profound reservations" on what he thought obvious weak points in the text, especially if they were judged in the light of the present situation. First, he objected to the terminology which groups together all the Eastern Churches, the true Orthodox as he sees his, the Uniates, that is those of Eastern Rite who joined Rome and the Ancient Churches in the East.

Secondly, the Patriarch made mention of the "paternalist tone" of the document which judges everything "by the measure of the truth of the See of Rome."

Bartholomew I had difficulty with certain suggestions made by the Pope about mutual recognition of saints and the cohabitation of Orthodox and Catholic monastic communities. He thought it presupposed a synodal act which Catholics and Orthodox were not yet to perform. There was need for clarification of ecclesiology.

The Patriarch thought that the idea of "twinning" between dioceses, parishes and communities was realistic, provided that such twinnings go beyond the social and cultural level.

As to the Pope's request for pardon for the mistakes of the past, Bartholomew had this to say: "One must praise the Pope when he calls Roman Catholics to recognize their own errors, committed at the expense of non-Catholics, something which has been done, as is known, by some of his eminent, even immediate, predecessors. We think that every Orthodox leader will have no difficulty in calling their faithful to recognize their errors and even their wrongs, against any one in the right, provided that it is not simply a rhetorical expression with a view to impressing. For, assuredly, we in our liturgical texts, we celebrant and faithful, recognize our unworthiness and without ambiguity we express the 'mea culpa, mea maxima culpa,' but unfortunately this remains, at least until now, a liturgical formula and only that, that is a stock phrase, which offends God and those who truly believe in him more than it satisfies him."

Reflections of the Ecumenical Patriarchate on its Understanding and Vision of the World Council of Churches on the Eve of the Third Millennium

1. This memorandum constitutes the due response of the Ecumenical Patriarchate to the letter of Dr. Konrad Raiser, General Secretary of the World Council of Churches, sent to the member-churches on the 10th of July, 1993. In that letter, the General Secretary had raised five fundamental questions pertaining to the nature of the World Council of Churches and its future orientation, and had asked the member-churches to formulate their view point. The initiative was timely and imposed, precisely after fifty years of a fertile, multi-faceted and productive activity, even if this very activity, from time to time and in various occasions, has been the object of reservations, criticism, and disagreements. The forthcoming 8th Assembly, coinciding with the fiftieth anniversary of the World Council of Churches, offers a unique opportunity for an evaluation of the Council's work and for a definition of its future orientation.

   It is with pleasure that the Ecumenical Patriarchate attempts this evaluation, and it is with good intention that it offers an objective formulation of its reflections and its vision concerning the future of an institution closely related to the contemporary ecclesiastical reality.

2. The qualification of the World Council of Churches in its Constitution as a "fellowship of churches" suggests that this institution is primarily an instrument at the disposal of the Churches, and not of any other organization or movement. As such, it has the end of assisting the Churches in their effort to promote the cause of the so much desired Christian unity. It also fosters a productive cooperation of its members, aiming at responding to the manifold problems and needs of the contemporary human persons and of all of life.

3. The term "communion" — an ecclesiological expression par excellence, as well as a Eucharistic term — which has been used throughout the twentieth century and, particularly, — we would even say with a certain emphasis — after the Fifth World Conference of Faith and Order in Santiago de Compostela, gives probably to the outsiders a wrong impression concerning the nature of the relationship and cooperation between Churches and Confessions within the World Council of Churches. The present reality in the World Council of Churches is, at least, a strange one. Within the Council coexist and cooperate Churches, and not only Churches, but also Confessions and other Christian entities. Therefore, any definition of the ecclesial character of all its members becomes almost impossible, given the fact that the criteria for membership, criteria based on numbers of faithful, organization or administration, are neither adequate, nor sufficiently clear, nor ecclesiologically unquestionable. Obviously, we refer here to those Christian entities which originate from or are the products of different historical, ecclesiological, theological and even cultural traditions and, therefore, can not be in Eucharistic communion with each other and, what is even more difficult, can not be in communion with Churches, such as the Orthodox Church for which strict and detailed ecclesiological prescriptions apply.

    Within the World Council of Churches, Churches and Confessions constitute a "fellowship" which, according to the same Constitution of the Council calls "the churches to the goal of visible unity in one faith and in one eucharistic fellowship expressed in worship and in common life in Christ, and to advance towards that unity in order that the world may believe" (III, 1). This "eucharistic fellowship" — we have to admit — is not a reality yet, while everything in the Council is in evolution. Nevertheless, after fifty years of fruitful cooperation within the World Council of Churches, its members are obliged to clarify the meaning and the extent of the fellowship they experience in it, as well as the ecclesiological significance of "koinonia," which is, precisely, the purpose and the aim of the World Council of Churches, and not the given reality.

4. Relationships between Churches and Confessions which cooperate within the Council have a distinctive nature and character, which is sufficiently indicated in the Toronto Statement: within the Council, Churches and Confessions reflect together, work together and walk together, aiming at Christian unity and the service of the contemporary humanity. For this reason, the Ecumenical Patriarchate considers that both the World Council of Churches and the ecumenical movement in general contribute to and serve the ecclesiological meaning of Christian unity, that is their primary object and raison d'etre are the restoration of unity in the Church.

5. The World Council of Churches has been rightly considered as the privileged instrument of the ecumenical movement: it constitutes the forum in which its member-churches can freely cooperate, fully defend their own tradition, and develop their multiform ecumenical activities on the ground of their own ecclesial identity, their tradition and their dogmatic teaching. Experience has shown, however, that, in the last twenty years, the bi-lateral relations between Churches and the multiplication of ecumenical and inter-confessional organizations or movements, which serve also the cause of Christian unity, compel the member-churches certainly to consider the World Council of Churches as the privileged and yet not the unique or exclusive instrument of the one ecumenical movement.

6. The assertion in the above paragraph 5 certainly prompts the Churches to have a new vision of the World Council of

Churches as an instrument and coordinating center of the ecumenical movement. It would be desirable, therefore, to ensure, in a foreseeable future, a closer coordination between the World Council of Churches and the Regional Ecumenical Organizations and this in order to avoid any waste in energy, human forces and material resources, especially taking into consideration the fact that it is now repeatedly affirmed that all Church Councils in the world (the World Council, as well as Regional and National Councils) serve the one and the same ecumenical idea. A closer relationship and cooperation between the World Council of Churches and other Councils — without excluding the degree of internal autonomy these Councils claim for themselves — could become beneficial not only in the promotion of Christian unity, but also in the diakonia of the fellow human persons.

7. During its fifty years of existence, the World Council of Churches has increased numerically, counting today approximately three hundred and thirty members. As we have already observed, however (paragraph 3), there is a great lack of homogeneity between the Council's members, not only as far as theology, ecclesiology, sacraments, tradition, etc. are concerned, but also as far as their stand vis-a-vis problems of the contemporary society. This became obvious during recent ecumenical conferences or assemblies of the World Council of Churches. There is no doubt that the readiness of various Churches, Confessions and other Christian entities to join the Council affirms the interest they manifest in the work undertaken by the Council. Nevertheless, in our effort to formulate a new vision for the World Council of Churches we can not avoid to raise the following question: what, in the coming years, will be the significance of the adherence to the Council of new Confessions, of small entities and of other ecclesiastical streams which today grow and develop at the expense of historical member-churches of the World Council of Churches, and not necessarily only at the expense of the Orthodox? Therefore, the Ecumenical Patriarchate considers that, together with the new vision about the World Council of Churches, it is necessary to

formulate some new, clearly theological and ecclesiological criteria for membership.

This is a fundamental request of the Ecumenical Patriarchate, and — we are sure — of all the Autocephalous Orthodox Churches and, presumably, of many other member-churches and Churches in working relations with the World Council of Churches — among which one should certainly include the Roman Catholic Church. We consider, therefore, that this should constitute an immediate priority for the Council, in order not to jeopardize its future, placing itself under question or self-contradiction.

8. As it was already observed, the World Council of Churches is an instrument of the ecumenical movement. The space in which it moves and acts is the "oikoumene." Nevertheless, the Ecumenical Patriarchate, and the Orthodox Church in general, consider that the technical term "ecumenical movement," which is used for more than seventy years in Christian circles, should not lose its original meaning. The joint activities of Christians, particularly their encounter with other faiths or ideological streams certainly take place within the wider framework of oikoumene, and they constitute expressions of the ecumenical movement. But surely they are not its primary scope. This is why, we believe, this technical term "ecumenical movement" should express the effort which aims at Christian unity only. In this respect there should be transparency at the level of terminology in use, in order to avoid any misrepresentations and misunderstandings.

9. The World Council of Churches always, and even before its official founding, namely when the ecumenical movement was focusing on the inter-church movements of the first decades of our century, — with the exception probably of "Faith and Order, which moved and continues to move on a specific theological ground — , dealt with a variety of issues directly relating to the life and problems of contemporary society and tried in many ways to find appropriate solutions. This multi-faceted and God-pleasing activity of the Council was highlighted by

the Ecumenical Patriarchate in the Message it issued in 1973, on the occasion of the 25th anniversary of the World Council of Churches. This diakonia of the Council was also recognized on a Pan-orthodox level in 1986 by the 3rd Preconciliar Panorthodox Conference. Today's situation in the world, sufferings caused by wars, social injustices, ethnic rivalries, and whatever offends the human person, this very "icon" of God, compel the Council to continue acting, on the basis of theological presuppositions, in the fields of diakonia, social welfare, justice, peace, defense of human rights, and the protection of the entire God's creation.

10. The Ecumenical Patriarchate, caring also for the spiritual and material growth of the Orthodox Churches in Eastern Europe and the Middle East, severely tormented for many decades, expresses to the World Council of Churches deep gratitude for its manifold assistance towards these Churches. As the Orthodox rightly remarked during the consultation about the common vision and understanding of the World Council Churches, held last June at the Orthodox Center of Chambesy, the Council, even during the difficult times of totalitarian regimes in Central and Eastern Europe "had began to speak and act on matters of peace, justice and human rights related to particular conditions in which the local Orthodox Churches involved were not free to articulate their position or to affect the situation." The Ecumenical Patriarchate, therefore, believes that the World Council of Churches, in any future programmatic activities beyond the next Assembly, should not neglect the field of diakonia, because this particular aspect of its activity transfigures into action whatever we debate on academic levels and consolidates the fellowship we experience in it.

11. World developments indicate that in the forthcoming millennium Churches will be facing situations tending to deteriorate the relationship between states, nations, races, religions. This was particularly emphasized by the Orthodox Primates during our recent summit meeting in Patmos, in September 1995. This is why the World Council of Churches should be always vigi-

lant and offer to its member-churches every possible assistance in their effort to become agents of peace, stability, and fraternity. In this connection, the Ecumenical Patriarchate wishes to underline that one factor of instability, insecurity, and enmity is the increasing phenomenon of aggressive activity by various sectarian or para-religious groups around the globe. This is why, it considers that the combat of this phenomenon, which encourages and sharpens all sorts of fundamentalist tendencies and tensions in inter-Christian or inter-faith relations, as well as the combat of the related problem of proselytism, should be one of the basic priorities of the Council in the years ahead of us.

12. The Ecumenical Patriarchate always gave and continues to give a particular importance to the theological research conducted in the framework of Unit I, particularly within the Commission of "Faith and Order," as well as in other programmatic clusters, such as the ones dealing with mission and evangelism. It is a fact that the theological research, even if it has progressed considerably during the last fifty years, was not in a position to bear concrete results able to lead us towards Christian unity. Probably because of insurmountable difficulties due to the lack of theological and ecclesiological homogeneity of those conversing in the WCC, fundamental themes, such as the Holy Tradition, ecclesiology, conciliarity, ordained ministry, mysteriology, particularly the sacraments of baptism and Eucharist, were not adequately advanced. This fact should not discourage us. Because, even if the theological dialogue advances with extremely slow steps, nothing prevents the member-churches from envisioning, for the post-Harare period, a World Council of Churches able to ensure a harmonious cooperation of all Christian forces in the moral, social, missionary, and diaconal fields, no matter what their basic doctrinal differences are, as the Ecumenical Patriarchate was stressing seventy years ago through its very well known 1920 Encyclical.

In concluding, we wish to underline that one of the visions the Ecumenical Patriarchate has for the World Council of Churches, is the evolution of the Council on the ground of a more rigorous ecclesiological basis and presuppositions, as we already mentioned above. This would contribute to the upgrading of its nature and it would, at the same time, facilitate the definition of the fellowship experienced in it by its member-churches.

The above reflections are submitted by the Ecumenical Patriarchate in great esteem and love in Christ.

Phanar, November 30, 1995
Feast of Saint Andrew, the Apostle

Appendix IV

Church Councils

General assemblies of the Church's hierarchy, officially convened to decide matters of doctrine or observance are known as Ecumenical Councils; the word has not the sense that it has in the ecumenical movement, which aims at Christian unity. In the future to which we look in hope, Church councils will have very great importance. Thanks to the initiative of Pope John XXIII in convening the Second Vatican Council and to the pastoral aim which he wished it to serve, thanks to the worldwide media interest and to a unique sequel, people have now some idea of this kind of religious event. The sequel was the immediate translation of the Council documents, Constitutions, Decrees and Declarations into vernacular languages. Another unique feature of the Council which may have promoted interest in it was the presence in Rome, for the first time, of representatives of the other Christian Churches and communions. They were Observers without the right to speak or vote in the conciliar meetings, but with considerable scope to exert indirect influence.

There were Orthodox representatives among them, those from Moscow being the first to reach the Eternal City. How do the Orthodox regard Ecumenical Councils? Their official attitude binds them to the first seven. So far in the Church there have been twenty-one; the meeting of the Apostles and elders described in Chapter XV of the Acts of the Apostles is taken as a prototype of the later assemblies; it is not included in the twenty-one.

The first eight ecumenical councils were convened by the Roman and later the Byzantine emperors. This surprises us nowadays. It is to be understood in the light of Church/state relations then existing; they were closely united and the emperor enjoyed a privileged position since it was Constantine who gave the Church freedom, ending three centuries of persecution.

These early council differ in importance from those that followed. St. Pope Gregory the Great compared the first four to the four gospels, because they taught the essential truths of our religion, the Holy Trinity and the Incarnation. The four which succeeded were also distinctive. Let us briefly consider the first seven by which the Orthodox are bound: all like the eight were held in the East. Nicaea, 325 A.D. solemnly, against the Arians, defined that the Son was consubstantial with the Father. The hero of the day was St. Athanasius of Alexandria. Constantinople I, 381, defined the divinity of the Holy Spirit. Ephesus, 431, approved, led by St. Cyril of Alexandria, the title *Theotekos*, Mother of God, for the Blessed Virgin Mary: this is her richest and most meaningful privilege. Chalcedon, 451, influenced by an important letter from Pope Leo the Great, taught that in Christ there were two natures and one person. Constantinople II, 553, condemned those seeking to continue the heresy repudiated at Chalcedon. Constantinople III, rejected the idea that there was only one will in Christ, the heresy of Monothelitism. Nicaea II, 787 A.D., condemned the heresy of Iconoclasm, the theory that images of the Lord, His Blessed Mother and the angels and saints were not justified: a phase of ferocity during which monks especially were persecuted.

After the break of 1054, attempts were made in western Councils to work out a reunion, at the Second Council of Lyons, 1274 and the Council of Florence, 1439. They were not accepted in Constantinople and councils held there in 1454 and 1484 formally rejected them.

There was no Orthodox participation in the Latin councils of the subsequent centuries, Trent, for example in the sixteenth and Vatican I in the nineteenth. It was in the latter that dogmas were defined, on papal infallibility and primacy, which caused problems for the Orthodox.

Declaration of the joint International Commission for theological dialogue between the Catholic Church and the Orthodox Church.

Introduction

1. At the request of the Orthodox Church, the normal sequence of theological dialogue with the Catholic Church was interrupted so that the question known as "uniatism" could be immediately approached.

2. As regards the method which has been called "uniatism," it was declared at Freising (June 1990) that "we reject it as a means of seeking unity, because it is opposed to the common tradition of our Churches."

3. In regard to the Eastern Catholic Churches, it is clear that they have, as part of the Catholic Communion, the right to exist and act in response to the spiritual needs of their faithful.

4. The document drawn up at Arricia by the joint coordinating committee (June 1991) and completed at Balamand (June 1993) shows the method we choose in the actual search for

full communion, giving also the reasons for excluding "uniatism" as a method.

5. This document comprises two parts: a) Ecclesiological principles, and b) Practical rules.

Ecclesiological Principles

6. The division between the Churches of the East and the West not only has never quenched the desire for the unity willed by Christ, but frequently this situation opposed to the nature of the Church has been for many an opportunity of achieving a more lively consciousness of the need there is to accomplish this unity so as to be faithful to the Lord's commandment.

7. Through the centuries varying attempts have been made to re-establish this unity. They sought to attain this goal by different ways, at times conciliar, in accord with the political, historic, theological and spiritual situation of each epoch. Unfortunately, none of these efforts succeeded in re-establishing full communion between the Church of the West and the Church of the East, and at times they even hardened the opposing positions.

8. During the last four centuries in different regions of the Orient, initiatives were taken from within certain Churches and under pressure from external elements, to re-establish communion between the Church of the East and the Church of the West. The initiatives led to the union of certain communities with the See of Rome, and entailed, as a consequence, a break in communion with their mother churches of the East. That took place not without the intrusion of extra-ecclesial interests. Thus were born the Catholic Oriental Churches, and thus a situation was created which became a source of conflicts and sufferings, first for the Orthodox, but also for Catholics.

9. Whatever about the intention and the genuineness of the will to be faithful to the commandment of the Lord, "That they may be one," one must note that the re-establishment of unity

between the Church of the East and the Church of the West has not been attained, and that the division persists, envenomed by these initiatives.

10. The situation thus created was in effect to give rise to tensions and oppositions. Progressively, in the decades following these unions, missionary activity put among its priorities, the effort to convert other Christians, individually or in groups, to have them return to one's own Church. To justify this tendency, which was a source of proselytism, the Catholic Church developed the theological outlook by which it set itself forward as the sole depository of salvation. In reaction, the Orthodox Church, in turn, came to adopt the same outlook, according to which, salvation was to be found only with her. To assure the salvation of "separated brethren," it happened that Christians were re-baptized and the demands of the religious freedom of persons and of their act of faith were forgotten, at the time little importance was attached to such things.

11. On the other hand, some civil authorities made attempts to bring back Eastern Catholics to the Church of their forefathers. To this end, when the opportunity was available, they did not hesitate to use objectionable means.

12. Because of the way in which Catholics and Orthodox see themselves anew in their relation to the mystery of the Church, and are again finding themselves as sister Churches, this form of missionary apostolate just described, known as "uniatism" is no longer acceptable neither as a practical method, or as a model of the unity sought by our Churches.

13. In effect, especially since the Panorthodox conferences and the Second Vatican Council, the rediscovery and the development of the idea of the Church as communion, as much by Orthodox as by Catholics, has radically changed perspectives and attitudes.

On one side and the other it is recognized that what Christ entrusted to his Church — the profession of apostolic faith, participation in the same Sacraments, especially in the unique priesthood celebrating the unique sacrifice of Christ, the apostolic succession of bishops — cannot be considered the exclusive property of one of our Churches. In this context, it is evident that all re-baptism is ruled out.

14. This is the reason why the Catholic Church and the Orthodox Church mutually recognize themselves as sister Churches, together responsible for the maintenance of the Church of God in fidelity to the divine plan, especially in what concerns unity. According to the words of Pope John Paul II, the ecumenical effort of the sister Churches of the East and the West, based on dialogue and prayer seeks perfect, total communion which will be neither absorption nor fusion but encounter in truth and love (cf. Slavorum Gentes, I., 27).

15. While respecting the inviolable freedom of persons and the universal obligation to follow the demands of conscience, there is no question in the effort to re-establish unity, or seeking conversion of persons from one Church to another to ensure their salvation. What matters is to realize together the will of Christ for those who are his and the Plan on his Church through common search between Churches, for complete agreement on the content of the faith and its implications. This effort is pursued in the ongoing theological dialogue. The present document marks a necessary stage in this dialogue.

16. The Catholic eastern Churches who have wished to re-establish full communion with the See of Rome and are thereto faithful, have the rights and obligations which are linked with this communion to which they belong. To rule their attitude towards Orthodox Churches they have the principles set forth buy the Second Vatican Council and given effect by the Popes who specified the practical consequences in different documents published since then. These Churches then must be brought into the dialogue of charity, in mutual respect and revived reciprocal confidence, at the local and university levels, and they must enter theological dialogue with all its practical implications.

17. In this atmosphere, the preceding considerations and the practical rules which follow, to the degree that they are really accepted and faithfully observed, are capable of leading to a just and definitive solution of the difficulties occasioned by these eastern Catholic Churches for the Orthodox Church.

18. In regard to this, Pope Paul VI had stated in his address at the Phanar in July, 1967, "that it is on the leaders and hierarchy of the Churches that it devolves to lead the Churches on the way that will bring them to a refound full communion. They must do this while recognizing and respecting each other as pastors of the part of Christ's flock entrusted to them, being attentive to the cohesion and growth of the People of God and avoiding everything that could cause a break or confusion in its ranks" (Tomos Agapis, n. 172). In this spirit Pope John Paul II and Ecumenical Patriarch Dimitrios together made this explicit statement: "We reject every form of proselytism, every attitude which could be or be seen to be a lack of respect..."

19. Mutual respect between Churches which are in difficult situations will increase notably to the degree that they follow the practical rules hereafter.

20. These rules will not resolve the problems which weigh on us if there is not first on each side a will to pardon, based on the Gospel, and at the heart of the constant effort towards renewal, a desire ceaselessly revived to recover the full communion which existed for more than a millennium between our Churches. It is here that the dialogue of love must enter with an intensity and perseverance ever renewed, for it alone can overcome mutual misunderstanding, and it is the climate necessary for a more profound theological dialogue which will clear the way for full communion.

21. The first step is to end everything which could maintain discord, contempt or hatred between the Churches. The authorities of the Catholic Church will to this end help the eastern Catholic Churches and their communities to prepare full com-

munion between the Catholic and Orthodox Churches. The authorities of the Orthodox Church will act in like manner with their faithful. Thus the extremely complex situation which arose in central and eastern Europe, both for Catholics and Orthodox, can be handled in both charity and justice.

22. The pastoral activity of the Catholic Church both Latin and Oriental no longer seeks to have the faithful pass from one Church to another; that it no longer aims at proselytism among the Orthodox. It aims at meeting the spiritual needs of its own faithful and has no wish to expand at the expense of the Orthodox Church. In these perspectives, in order to avoid distrust and suspicion, it is necessary to have reciprocal information on the different pastoral projects, that thus between the bishops and officials of our Churches cooperation may begin and develop.

23. The history of relations between the Orthodox Church and the eastern Catholic Churches has been marked by persecutions and sufferings. Whatever these sufferings and their causes may have been, they warrant no triumphalism; no one can take the glory in them or use them as an argument to accuse or belittle the other Church. God alone knows his true witness. Whatever the past has been, it must be left to the mercy of God, and all the energies of the Churches must be bent to ensuring that the present and future are more in keeping with the will of Christ for those who belong to him.

24. On one side and the other also bishops and all those in official positions must scrupulously allow for the religions freedom of the faithful. These must be able to express their opinion freely on being consulted or in growing to this purpose. Religious freedom really demands that, especially in situations of conflict, the faithful be able to set forth their choice and decide without external pressure whether they wish to be in communion with the Orthodox Church or with the Catholic Church. Religious freedom would be violated when, under the cover of financial aid, an attempt would be made to attract the faithful of the other Church by promising them, for example, educa-

tion and the material advantages lacking in their own Church.

In this context social help must be organized in agreement, as every philanthropical activity, to avoid the appearance of new suspicions.

25. In other respects the necessary respect for Christian liberty — one of the most precious gifts received in Christ, should no be an occasion for initiating, without previous consultation with the authorities in these Churches, pastoral projects which would also involve the faithful of these Churches. Not only should all pressure, of whatever kind, be excluded, but respect for consciences, coming from a genuine motive of faith, is one of the principles ruling the pastoral care of the authorities in the two Churches and should be the object of their consultation.

26. This is why open dialogue must be sought and undertaken in the first place between those who have responsibility in the Churches on the spot. The leaders of each of the communities involved will set up local commissions with equal representation, or will ensure the efficacy of those in existence, to find solutions for concrete problems and to have these solutions applied in truth and love, in justice and peace.

If agreement cannot be reached at a local level, the questions should be referred to the higher authorities working as joint commissions.

27. Distrust would more easily disappear if both sides condemned violence wherever communities practice it against the communities of a sister Church. As His Holiness Pope John Paul II asks, in his letter of May 31, 1991, all violence and every kind of pressure must be avoided so that freedom of conscience is respected.

It is for the leaders of communities to help their faithful to deepen their loyalty to their own Church and its tradition, and to teach them to avoid not only violence, be it physical, verbal or moral but everything which could lead to contempt for other Christians, to hostile witness, ridiculing the work of salvation which is reconciliation in Christ.

28. Faith in sacramental reality implies that one respects all the liturgical celebrations of other Churches. Use of violence to take over a place of worship contradicts this conviction. This, on the contrary, demands that in certain circumstances one should facilitate the celebration by other Churches, making one's own church available to them, by an agreement allowing alternative celebration at different times in the same building.

   More than that, gospel ethics demands that one abstain from declaration or manifestations liable to perpetuate a state of conflict and to harm dialogue. Does St. Paul not exhort us to be welcoming to one another, as Christ was for us to the glory of God? (cf. Rom 15:7)

29. Bishops and priests have the duty before God of respecting the authority the Holy Spirit has given to bishops and priests of the other Church, and to that end, to avoid interfering in the spiritual life of the faithful of this Church. When cooperation becomes necessary for their good, the leaders are required to act in concert, fixing clear bases, known to all, for this mutual aid, acting then frankly and openly, respecting the sacramental discipline of the other Church.

   In this context, to avoid all misunderstanding, and to develop trust between the two Churches, it is necessary that Catholic and Orthodox bishops of the same territory, should consult each other before implementation of Catholic pastoral projects, which entail the creation of new structures in regions traditionally dependent on the jurisdiction of the Orthodox Church, this to avoid parallel pastoral activities which would risk becoming quickly competitive and even conflicting.

30. To prepare future relations between the two Churches, going beyond the out of date ecclesiology of return to the Catholic Church bound up with the problem with which this document is dealing, special attention will be given to the preparation of future priests, and of all those in any way involved in apostolic activity exercised where the other Church is traditionally rooted. Their education must be objectively positive in regard

to the other Church. All must be instructed in the apostolic succession of the other Church and of the genuineness of its sacramental life.

In the same way an honest and overall view of history should be given to all, proceeding towards a historiography which is in agreement and even common between the two Churches. This will help to dispel prejudices and will avoid history being used in a polemical manner. This view will give an awareness that the wrongs of the separation were shared, leaving deep wounds on one side and the other.

31. We shall remember the warning of the apostle Paul to the Corinthians (1 Cor. 6:1-7) advising Christians to settle their disagreements by means of fraternal dialogue, which would save them from relying on the intervention of civil authorities for the practical solution of the problems which arise between Churches of local communities.

    This bears especially on the possession or restitution of ecclesiastical goods. These must not be founded solely on past situations, or rely entirely on general juridical principles, but must take account of the complexity of present pastoral realities and of local circumstances.

32. In this spirit the re-evangelization of our secularized world can be faced together. An effort will be made to give the mass-media unbiased news, especially to the religious press, to that inexact or tendentious information will be eschewed.

33. It is necessary that the Churches should associate to express gratitude and respect for all those, known and unknown, bishops, priests or faithful, Orthodox, eastern or Latin Catholics, who have suffered, confessed their faith and witnessed to their fidelity to the Church, and, in general, to all Christians without discrimination who have suffered persecution.

    Their sufferings summon us to unity, and to give, in our turn, a common witness to answer the prayer of Christ, "that all may be one, that the world may believe" (Jn. 17:21).

34. The Joint International Commission for Theological Dialogue between the Catholic Church and the Orthodox Church, at a plenary meeting in Balamand, strongly recommends that these practical rules be implemented by our Churches, including the Eastern Catholic Churches, called to take part in this dialogue which must be pursued in the serene atmosphere necessary to its progress, towards the re-establishment of full communion.

35. By excluding for the future all proselytism, and every will to increase the number of Catholics at the expense of the Orthodox Church, the Commission hopes that it has eliminated the obstacle which pushed certain autocephalous Churches to suspend their participation in the theological dialogue, and that the Orthodox Church will be able to come back fully to continue the theological work so happily begun.

Balamand, Lebanon
June 23, 1993

Appendix VI

I

BARTHOLOMEW

BY THE MERCY OF GOD ARCHBISHOP OF CONSTANTINOPLE, THE NEW ROME AND ECUMENICAL PATRIARCH PATRIAR- CHAL AND SYNODICAL ACT CONCERNING THE RE-ACTIVATION OF THE PATRIARCHAL AND SYNODICAL TOMOS OF 1923 REGARDING THE ORTHODOX METROPOLITANATE OF ESTONIA

"It is customary to change the boundaries of the Churches as political entities and administrations change," declared Photios the Great, wise among the Patriarchs.

Because the Orthodox Christians residing in Estonia and constituting an honorable segment of the Estonian Nation have sought spiritual protection and the settlement of their ecclesiastical affairs by the Most Holy Church of Constantinople, the historical Mother Church of all the Orthodox people in Eastern and Central Europe, She, as a tender Mother, accepting the free and unanimous request of her children, acknowledged and blessed the autonomy of the Orthodox Church in Estonia under the spiritual supervision of the Ecumenical Patriarchate through the Patriarchal and Synodical Tomos issued by our ever-memorable predecessor, Ecumenical Patriarchate Meletios IV, in July, 1923.

However, twenty years later, the violent destruction of the freedom and the independence of the Estonian State occurred, at which time the ecclesiastical autonomy of the Orthodox Christians in Estonia was also violently destroyed. Since their lawful Metropolitan Alexander together with many clerics and thousands of lay people fled to Sweden in March 1944, the autonomous Church of Estonia was made subject to the Church of Russia, following the contracted political change of the time, though not according to canonical order.

The Most Holy Apostolic Patriarchal and Ecumenical Throne, being the guardian of canonical exactness, refusing to accept the events caused by uncanonical force and tyranny, has long continued to regard the autonomy of the Estonian Orthodox Church as being in effect and represented canonically by those Orthodox Estonians who fled to live in exile outside the then Soviet Union. In this spirit, the Mother Church of Constantinople in 1978, prompted by ecclesiastical economy, responding with brotherly love to the request of the Church of Russia, due to the circumstances of the times, proclaimed the Tomos of 1923 inoperative through a Patriarchal and Synodical Act. This means that the Tomos could not be enforced within Estonia which at that time comprised part of the Soviet Union; the Tomos, however, was not regarded as being void, invalid or revoked.

But already, by 1991, Estonia, having become a free and independent state, demands, in accordance to the practice for all Orthodox nations, that the former autonomous status of the Orthodox Church in Estonia be restored through the reactivation of the Patriarchal and Synodical Tomos of 1923, which calls for returning to the fatherland, where she had been abolished, the exiled Autonomous Estonian Apostolic Orthodox Church, as it was officially called from 1935 onwards.

Accordingly, the Most Holy Mother Church of Constantinople — empowered by the strength of the Divine and Sacred Canons, numbers 9 and 17 of the holy 4th Ecumenical Synod in Chalcedon which state: "If any bishop or clergyman has a dispute with the Metropolitan of the same province, let him apply either to the Exarch of the diocese, or to the throne of the imperial capital Constantinople, and let it be tried before him" (Canon 9) and "If anyone has been unjustly treated by his own Metropolitan, let him complain to the Exarch of the diocese, or let him have his case tried before the throne of Constantinople, according as he may choose" (Canon 17); in addition, the 34th Canon of the Holy Apostles which exhorts the Churches of different nations, and especially those in free and independent States, should be formed into autonomous or autocephalous Churches under their particular bishop — has accepted the rightful request of the Orthodox Christians in Estonia and of the honorable government of the Estonian Apostolic Orthodox Church as it was before 1940, as an autonomous Church under the jurisdiction of the Ecumenical Patriarchate.

Therefore, our Modesty, together with the Most Reverend and Right Honorable Metropolitans, our dearly beloved brothers in the Holy Spirit and concelebrants in Christ — having deliberated synodically, trustworthily taking care of the governance and the administration of all ecclesiastical matters and having foresight of what is proper, as has been the canonical custom from time immemorial that the Most Holy Ecumenical Throne has the right to adapt and to provide for the constitution and foundation of the Churches, appropriately addressing the needs of the times and the good estate of the entire assembly always striving for the harmonious and advantageous portrayal and governance of the local and the universal — declare anew that the Patriarchal and Synodical Tomos of 1923 regarding the Orthodox Metropolitanate of Estonia is reactivated in all its articles. We also recognize as the lawful successors of the Estonian Apostolic Orthodox Church those who accepted the Tomos and unceasingly preserved her canonical continuation.

At the same time, we state that, having in mind the concerns of His Beatitude our Brother Patriarch Alexy of Moscow and all Russia regarding the immigrant Orthodox faithful in Estonia of Russian descent who were established there during the period when Estonia constituted a part of what was then the Soviet Union, we declare our firm desire that their unhindered ecclesiastical life be ensured, consisting of an integral unit of the Estonian Autonomous Church, organized under their own Russian-speaking bishop, in the hope that their canonical and legal situation may be settled in a spirit of love and peace, and in the understanding of the brotherly unity of all Orthodox peoples.

Wherefore, we issued our present Patriarchal and Synodical Act as declaration and assurance and as permanent representation of the matters considered and decided upon ecclesiastically regarding the reactivation of the Patriarchal and Synodical Tomos of 1923, drawn up and signed in this Sacred Codex of our Most Holy Great Church of Christ, and a same and exact copy released and sent to the designated Locum Tenens of the Orthodox Autonomous Apostolic Church of Estonia, the Most Reverend Archbishop John of Karclia and all Finland, our beloved brother in the Lord, to be placed in the archives of the Autonomous Church of Estonia.

In the year of our Salvation, 1996, February 20

EPINEMESIS 4

[Seal of the Patriarch of Constantinople]   attests to this

Ioachim of Chalcedon	co-attests
Ieronymos of Rodopolis	co-attests
Symeon of Pringhiponneson	co-attests
Evangelos of Perga	co-attests
Kallinikos of Lystra	co-attests
Konstantinos of Derkon	co-attests
Athanasios of Heliopolis and Theira	co-attests
Germanos of Tranoupolis	co-attests
Meliton of Philadelphia	co-attests

II

Your Beatitude, Most Holy Patriarch Alexy of Moscow and all Russia, our Modesty's most beloved and dear brother in Christ God and concelebrant: Embracing Your venerable Beatitude in the Lord, we greet you exuberantly.

Your most beloved and distinguished Beatitude's letter of February 6, 1996, indicates that so far You have not wanted to comprehend the truly peacemaking intentions of the Most Holy Mother Church of Constantinople regarding the matter of the Estonian Church. Instead, You, accuse the Ecumenical Patriarchate anew of transgressing the Holy Canons and hurl uncharacteristic threats at it and us, personally, which ought not to happen.

Until this point, our Church of Constantinople has deliberately avoided accusing the Most Holy Church of Russia. On the contrary, from the beginning the Church of Constantinople has tried to build a bridge over the psychological gap between the Orthodox Estonians and the Orthodox of Russia descent created during the Soviet occupation. We are mindful that the Russian Church was also tormented by the Soviet regime, and indeed for a longer period of time than the Church in Estonia, and we justify Your personal opposition, Beatitude and brother, on this issue, as being due to Your emotional bond with Your own homeland of Estonia.

But You, Beatitude and brother, and Your Church, while not responding to these endeavors of ours, continue to accuse both the Orthodox Estonians as an illicit assembly and us as interfering uncanonically in the internal matters of the Church of Russia. And all the while negotiations are in process, sometimes by publishing articles against us, sometimes by imposing the penalty of suspension of those clergymen in Estonia who have referred themselves to the Ecumenical Patriarchate, You are acting in a manner which clearly indicates that You are using the negotiations as a pretext to secure an indefinite extension thus greatly damaging the sacred cause of Orthodoxy in Estonia.

In addition, we need the to further declare the following:

1. In no way are you justified in considering the Orthodox Estonians guilty of an uncanonical act of insubordination towards their supposed canonical bishop, namely Archbishop Kornelios, since he constitutes the continuation of the violently accomplished overthrow in 1944 of the canonical order by the Stalinist Army. Then, as it is known and corroborated, the then canonical Metropolitan Alexander of Tallion and all Estonia was forced to flee abroad with 23 clergymen and 7000 lay people, while another 45 clerics were murdered or exiled. These things occurred when the persecutions against the Russian Church were already past, and Your predecessors, Sergios and Alexy I, accepted the just praise of Stalin for their heroic contribution in defending their fatherland against the German invaders. It is therefore obvious that this so honored Russian Church of that time was involved in the expulsion of the Orthodox Estonians

and benefitted from it in order to take over the territory of the Orthodox Estonian Church. The foundations of the Archdiocese of Archbishop Kornelios are not canonical and it is not right to invoke the divine and sacred Canons in this case.

2. But nor can the flock of Archbishop Kornelios be regarded as a continuation of the flock of the Estonian Apostolic Orthodox Church prior to 1940, since the greater majority of them are Russian immigrants who were coerced by Stalin to establish themselves *in masse* in Estonia in order to alter the ethnological composition of the population. How can a Church be called "Estonian" when it is made up of Russian immigrants?

3. In no way are You justified, Beatitude, in condemning the Orthodox Estonians of phyletism. They, as a race themselves, have the right, in accordance with the 34th Canon of the Holy Apostles, to constitute their own Church, having the bishops in their Church and the first among them from among their own race, especially since they constitute a sovereign and independent nation.

4. The Most Holy Church of Russia is not at all justified in accusing the Ecumenical Patriarchate of encroaching in the internal affairs of the Church of Russia while transgressing the Holy Canons. On the contrary, the Patriarchate of Russia during those years trespassed in countries under the spiritual jurisdiction of the Ecumenical Patriarchate, namely, Estonia, Hungary and elsewhere, always by the power of the Soviet Army. The Church of Russia did not at the time seek the opinion of the Ecumenical Patriarchate, nor was any respect shown it. The annexation of the Orthodox Church of Estonia into the Most Holy Church of Russia happened arbitrarily and uncanonically. And it is certain that events which are uncanonical at one particular time are never blessed, never seen as efficacious and never would they set a precedence.

5. Even if the issue were not one of a territory belonging to the spiritual jurisdiction of the Ecumenical Patriarchate according

to the strict interpretation of the Canons, it was still duty-bound to intervene; of course, not of its own volition, but if invited to do so by someone who has been wronged. The holy and God-bearing fathers in Canons 9 and 17 of the Holy Fourth Ecumenical Council in Chalcedon placed upon the Church of Constantinople the most onerous responsibility of adjudicating cases of other local Churches when called upon to do so. How great a weight this responsibility is is demonstrated by the issue at hand, when in defense of the small number of people who are Orthodox Estonians, the Ecumenical Patriarchate has to displease the Most Holy and cherished daughter Church of Russia. It does this precisely in defense of this small flock, not for personal gain, since the Ecumenical Patriarchate stands to gain nothing from this situation apart from the moral reward which comes from the gratitude of the Orthodox Estonians. The Ecumenical Patriarchate takes such action by exercising the obligation given to it by tradition and established custom and its responsibility to meet the needs of the Churches in particular circumstances and of Orthodox people everywhere.

6. Our Church was further surprised at the uneasiness of Your Beatitude regarding possible actions of the Ecumenical Patriarchate at the expense of the Orthodox faithful in Estonia of Russian descent. Do you believe, Most Honored Brother, that it is possible, while defending the downtrodden rights of the Orthodox Estonians that we as the Church of Constantinople would accept trampling the rights of the Russians in Estonia? Rather, the Ecumenical Throne can never forget that from it the great race of the Russians received the light of Christ and saving baptism. For many long centuries your ancestors have been children of those children. The Mother never stops loving her children, even when the children deny the Mother. Even if you, Most Blessed Brother, systematically refuse to refer to the fundamental historical significance of the Church, and You address her simply as "Elder Sister," still You, personally, were born in Estonia under the omophorion of the Church of Constantinople and as her child You were baptized and spent your childhood there.

We declare, then, before God and man, that the Orthodox faithful of Russian descent constitute for us beloved children of the Church, the same as are the Orthodox Estonians, and we are ready to protect them also, if necessary. So we desire the brotherly cooperation of all and reject every sort of unbrotherly action no matter what side it comes from.

Inevitably, the prolongation of uncertainty and the climate of mutual suspicion created by it brings about only harm and widens the chasm between the two groups of Orthodox brethren. In particular, the long-term abandonment of the Orthodox Estonians without the necessary ecclesiastical tutelage only propagates the danger that they will join other Christian Churches. For this reason we deemed it necessary and indeed imperative — since all our attempts for a peaceful resolution between the two Churches produced nothing for which You are at fault — to proceed in reactivating the Patriarchal and Synodical Tome of 1923, which the Patriarchal and Synodical Praxis of 1978 has made inoperative, but not invalid. If the Praxis of 1978 was enacted for the sake of smooth relations with the Patriarchate of Moscow, at which time Estonia still constituted a section of the then Soviet Union, the new Praxis is enacted at the request of the Orthodox Estonians who are of immediate concern and of their State, following the radical political change which occurred with the declaration of Estonian independence in 1991. A similar prior example lies before us, namely, the Russian Orthodox Parishes in Western Europe under the venerable Ecumenical Throne. The Ecumenical Patriarchate, as a token and proof of its sincere disposition towards the Patriarchate of Moscow, by a Praxis in 1965 released these parishes from its jurisdiction, although it was forced later to receive them once again at the persistent request of their members.

We hope that you understand, Beatitude and Brother, You and the Most Holy Russian Church around You, that the canonical Praxis to which we have proceeded in no way turns against the Orthodox in Estonia of Russian descent, but rather contributes to the alleviation of their ordeals as well. Besides, in our Patriarchal and Synodical Praxis, a copy of which is attached for Your information, there is specific mention of the situation of the Orthodox of Russian descent as You can testify.

In closing, embracing once again, Your beloved Beatitude as a brother in the Lord, we remain with unending love in Him and with special esteem.

February 24, 1996
Your most venerable Beatitude's
Beloved brother in Christ,
[signed: +Bartholomew of Constantinople]